EduMatch®:
Snapshot in Education (2017)
Volume 2:
Professional Practice

educational matchmaker

ISBN-10: 0692046402 | ISBN-13: 978-0692046401

EduMatch®:
Snapshot in Education (2017)
Volume 2:
Professional Practice

Contributing Authors
(by Order of Chapter):

CHRISTY CATE | CATHY WOLFE
JASON R. FALCONIO | STEPHAN HUGHES
FABIANA L. CASELLA | HEIDI CARR
BARBARA COTTER | STEPHANIE FILARDO
STEPHANIE D. JACOBS | KELLY GROTRIAN
MARIALICE B.F.X. CURRAN, PhD
JOSUE FALAISE, Ed.D. | DAN KREINESS
JASON B. ALLEN | MASON, M.Ed.
MIRACULE GAVOR | J. DEREK LARSON
SARAH THOMAS
Edited by Sarah Thomas

ISBN-10: 0692046402 | ISBN-13: 978-0692046401

ACKNOWLEDGMENTS

Thank you to the following chapter editors,
who helped to make this book possible:

Rachel Baughman (Ch. 5)
Christy Cate (Ch. 5)
Derek Larson (Chs. 2 & 7)
Dr. Jacie Maslyk (Ch. 12)
Tori Mazur (Ch. 8)
Katie McFarland (Ch. 9)
Kathleen Reardon (Ch. 4)
Rodney Turner (Chs. 1 & 15)

DEDICATION

This book is dedicated to the EduMatch® family of educators. Thank you to those of you who have been so willing to share, as we continue to learn and grow together.

CONTENTS

The Power of Connection in Lifelong Learning: An Elevator Approach to Education

Christy Cate and Cathy Wolfe

The Elevator Story - *Learning has minimal meaning unless it is experienced.*

> "No school, no reading,
> no writing, no elevators."
> ~ Shanti B.

Cathy from a Vox to Christy on April 22, 2017

One of the greatest challenges concerning our ESL standardized tests is that the content often has no real meaning for some of my students. When they come to this country, they are illiterate, even in their own language. They have never been to school anywhere before now. They have no idea how to write their name in their own language, let alone the English language. They have some wonderful things in their culture - pure, pristine air, they grew everything fresh, they are experts at farming. However, when they have to answer what seems like a simple test question with a picture of someone at an elevator with their finger on the "up" button, and the question is, "which way is he going?" they have *no idea*.

By the time they are ready for this level test, they have learned how to read and write some basic English. They understand and can use the words "up" and "down." But seeing those words in a picture of an elevator means *nothing* to them because they can't relate the picture to anything from their life experiences. Even though they have probably been on an elevator since coming to the US, they don't make the connection. No matter how many times we try to teach that concept from the picture, they keep missing the answer. Even when I put up and down arrow signs around the classroom, it doesn't seem to help them "read" the picture.

But one day, one of my volunteers, a retired elementary reading specialist shared an epiphany:

"They can't answer this question because they don't associate the picture with the actual experience of pushing buttons in an elevator. We need to take them on an elevator so they can push the buttons!"

We did that, and guess what? **They got it.**

Christy's epiphany that resulted: This "elevator" moment completely explains what learners (of all ages) experience regularly -- I know it, I can verbalize it, and I honestly DON'T GET IT! Ugh! And our current system of education is so focused on data derived from assessing the "I know it, and I can verbalize it" aspect. What Cathy is exemplifying in the "I don't get it!" aspect is the growth in learning point. Just like an elevator, when we experience learning... we go up, we go down, we get on, we get off, we wait, we feel uncomfortable, we ponder, and we finally arrive at the penthouse.

Meet Cathy

Cathy first began teaching in 1980, then jumped to the business world for 14 years before returning to the classroom. She has a unique instructional experience in that she teaches a multi-level ESL class for adults in Grand Haven, Michigan. Her students include a wide range of ages, cultures, first languages and educational

backgrounds. She has a passion for supporting
students to reach their learning goals and
embraces a flexible teaching style that is open to
"whatever works." She also loves technology and
is committed to infusing technology into her
classes in any way that enhances her students'
learning. In December 2015, she stepped onto the
ride of expanding her professional learning
network by joining Voxer groups mostly
populated with K12 educators.

Meet Christy

Christy grew up in a family of educators and
vowed that education would NOT be her destiny.
God, however, had other plans for her, and after
first starting out in the business world, she found
herself finally at home in a classroom in 1997.
Her business background gave her an edge in
technology use when tech tools hit the schools.
She eventually became an Instructional
Technology Specialist, and currently serves as a
Digital Innovation Consultant for 42 rural school
districts in West Texas. By chance, she happened
across a tweet in October of 2014 and stepped
onto the Voxer ride herself.

Cathy and Christy found themselves both in
EduMatch, established by innovator and educator
Sarah Thomas (see edumatch.org). This fast-

paced Voxer discussion group (just one of many platforms in which to participate with EduMatch) is filled with brilliant educators around the globe that collaborate daily, sharing growth, excitement, disappointment, advice, friendship, and experiences of learning for their students and themselves. Many smaller discussion groups have appeared over the years that surround specific topics, interests, and personalities. Often, individuals meet "on the side" to continue conversations one-on-one. That is how this unsuspecting elevator ride began...

Going up? Which floor, please?

(How we became friends who have never met face-to-face)

Cathy

I put a question out on the EduMatch Voxer group one day - Christy answered in a "side vox" specifically to me! We started up a dialogue that has grown over the last year and a half into an ongoing relationship -- coworkers, friends, really. I work on implementing and solidifying new tools that will enhance the learning experiences of my students. Christy is right there, supporting me on a daily (or multiple times per day) basis -- helping with problem-solving, providing ideas and suggestions, cheering me on, listening and responding to my reflections with Q&A, suggestions, and reflections of her own. The reflection piece is KEY for me -- it accelerates the implementation process and catalyzes ideas for new projects, as well as tweaks to current activities.

Christy

When I first became a regular participant in EduMatch on Voxer, there were maybe 15 members. As the group grew to two rooms with over 500 people in the first room, I learned quickly that voices come and go. New participants are enthusiastic and share often, until, like the rest of us, life gets busy, they join multiple groups, and they find it necessary to declare "Voxer bankruptcy." When I check in to find over 100 unread/unheard voxes, I often listen without responding in the big group. It was just such a moment that led me to message Cathy on the side. Having never met face-to-face is trivial in our modern culture. We are friends and colleagues, and it is Cathy's reflections, struggles, and growths that have likewise helped me to have an articulated voice for the teachers I work with in person.

Check out the amenities on the second floor!

(How our relationship affects the classroom)

Cathy

Even though Christy isn't physically in the classroom, her "presence" is felt every day as I implement new ideas and reflect on them almost daily in our ongoing Voxer conversation. My ESL classroom has literally transformed from a printed handout environment to a technology-based BYOD classroom, with a solid foundation in Google Classroom and Seesaw as our main organizational and digital portfolio tools.

Christy

Cathy is that educator I see each time I enter a campus building. Regardless of learning curves, learning styles, challenges, and red tape, it is rare that my presence is requested without the desire for a different approach to instruction as the outcome. I have replayed the tape recorder of Cathy's conversation more times than I can count in my mind when establishing relationships and trying to understand from where an educator's frustrations and needs might be coming. At times,

it is real, tangible examples from Cathy that I can
implement with local educators.

Is this your stop? Getting off here?

(Three examples of transformation in Cathy's classroom)

From large projector to BYOD

Starting point: Cathy, as teacher, would
manage a running doc (class notes for the day) in
real time from her computer and project onto a
large screen so all students could see. These doc
notes evolved based on students' meaning,
pronunciation issues, questions, and other factors.
Cathy added images on the fly as needed, and she
did all the typing of students' comments,
questions, conversations, et cetera - an effective,
teacher-centered approach. Cathy knew it could
be better, though.

Today: Cathy creates and dates the "doc of
the day" from a blank template. She might add
some content from previous classes that need
continued practice, but she leaves the doc mostly
blank so that students can collaborate in building
the lesson. Every student accesses the "doc of the
day" via Google Classroom. Students read and
follow along with the class doc from whatever

device they can access. Cathy, as teacher, continues to manage the doc and takes notes; *however,* students enter their own questions, write answers to others' questions, and collaborate on the doc directly via the "table" format. These collaborative class notes may evolve into a practiced conversation that is recorded in Seesaw (or in the future, on a Flipgrid or another TBD format).

Practice assessment material - from print to Google Forms Quiz

Starting point: Cathy, as teacher, prepared material targeted to teach concepts and vocabulary that students needed to learn for standardized tests. She prepared materials using a Google Doc. She then projected the doc on a large screen. Students followed along, practiced, asked questions, et cetera. She then printed the class notes for students to review at home if they wished, and gave printed practice questions and practice assessments. It worked! But could the practice be done more efficiently?

Today: Students get a shared Google Doc via Classroom on their devices. Cathy goes through the material with students the same as before, but with this method, students can look up unknown vocabulary words and enter them into the doc for the class (instead of depending on the teacher to do it). Students can make up their own practice sentences and type them into the doc (instead of dictating to the teacher).

When the practice is complete, students can take the practice assessment questions via a Google Forms Quiz. Both students and teacher can instantly see results and can immediately re-teach/review. It may seem like a small adjustment, but WOW! These students are also practicing tech skills that will translate into their daily lives.

Casual conversation to eBook via Book Creator

Starting point: Promoting and even assigning casual conversations among students are an essential part of the learning process. One day, Cathy noticed that two students had decorated each other's hands with henna. The other students noticed and were complimenting them and asking them questions. She realized a teachable moment was right before her, and the seeds for a collaborative project were planted.

Today: The casual conversation became a shared Google Doc, and the shared Google Doc has turned into an eBook with audio via these steps (notice the table format on the next page… such a format works well to keep content organized for students on a regular basis):

1 | Conversation among students.

2 | Created a table and generated more formal conversation with the group -- a mixture of students asking questions orally and/or writing them (depending on their skill level at writing questions in English).

3 | Students with experience and knowledge about henna answered questions - this began in class and continued at home.

4 | Olga G. and Fatima A. worked together to find photos and a video for the content generated in the Google Doc.

5 | Olga, Fatima, and teacher Cathy met after class to learn how to use the Book Creator app.
The students copied and pasted their text from the Google Doc to the book.
The students added their images and video.
The students refined their layout.

6 | The students practiced and then recorded audio.

7 | Shared as ePub > open in iBooks or read in
Book Creator via private link.

Oh! You're going down? No problem!

(Adjusting the path)

Cathy

What I have found in my instructional practice, is that the path to successfully implementing something new means CONSTANT adjustment. (My definition of "success" is measured by both progress AND completion of various practices -- try an idea, note what works and what doesn't work, and make changes.)

For instance, this year I wanted beginning students to be able to do a matching activity by drawing a line from a picture to its descriptive word on their devices. This is easy to do with paper and pencil, but I wanted them to be able to do this digitally as well. I also wanted those who can write but are slow typists to be able to annotate a photo, and/or write a few words or a sentence on a picture using their finger or stylus. There are many ways to do this, but they all involve introducing new apps (something I wasn't ready to do yet).

Christy suggested using the Camera Roll Markup feature since it's already on the iPad and the students were familiar with accessing photos on the Camera Roll. I explored it and found it very useful for myself as a quick way to annotate. However, in practice in the classroom, students found it awkward and even difficult to accomplish the desired outcome. Markup has a sequential "undo" feature, but it doesn't have a delete feature where you can tap on an element and delete just that element. After playing with it, I decided NOT to use it with students.

A few months later, Christy discovered and suggested wizer.me, which has the matching feature as a test question type. Since I was already focused on Google Forms, I decided to put the matching project on the back burner. I concluded that completing my transition from paper quiz questions to Google Forms was top priority and that additional tools would be explored further down the road. It has proven to be an excellent decision because now I have most of my assessment practice questions formatted into Google Forms Quizzes that students can easily access, and they feel comfortable with this process!

In fact, when transforming my quizzes from paper/pencil to Google Forms, the Doc to Form extension worked well and sped up the process significantly. However (brace yourself - I'm getting off on a different floor), some of the questions referred the student to a single paragraph of text. I asked Christy about the best way to adjust the font size for the question to minimize the scrolling issue, as I couldn't figure it out on my own. She confirmed that in Google Form's current version (as of February 2016), there was no easy way to do this and suggested a couple of workarounds. I tried them and finally decided that the most effective way was to adjust the font in a doc first, take a screenshot and bring the text into the form as an image.

Maria's Job

Maria is the receptionist at the Lake Shore Children's Clinic. She talks to patients and schedules appointments for them. She also uses the computer and answers the phone. She is very busy but she likes her job.

What is Maria's job?

doctor

patient

receptionist

Lakeshore

I'll Ride Down with You, and Then We'll Both Head Up

(Learning as an educator... and learning from the students!)

Cathy

I grow so much in the moments where I am the student, and those in my class teach me. We all learn together when students can solve problems that challenge me (the teacher), or identify a mistake that I've unknowingly made. Those moments provide a natural way for me to demonstrate that even as a teacher, I'm always learning, too, and that making mistakes is an integral part of the learning process.

A great example of this revolved around my efforts to digitize my pencil and paper quizzes with Google Docs and Forms. When I first discovered the Doc to Form extension, I was very excited to see how well it worked, so I started playing with some of the various question types. I accidentally put one of my experimental forms into a folder that I shared with all my students.

A student went into the folder and tried to take that unfinished quiz. She ran into problems, of course, and tried to explain to me in her minimal English that there were some mistakes in how I had set up the questions, but she was having a hard time conveying meaning. Her English isn't bad, but she talks fast and jumbles her words, and it was hard for me to understand what she was trying to say. Finally, I got the gist of the issue, and she was right. I hadn't meant for that format to be out there at all, but that's what happens when you're assessing, experimenting, and trying new things. So, I said to her, "I'm so glad you're here today, because you're giving me feedback that I really need about these forms."

I was trying to communicate to her that I was in a state of learning myself…and what do you know? It was more difficult than I imagined for me to convey an adequate meaning of mastering the skills myself. She initially didn't understand that I wasn't an expert and was in the learning process too. Making mistakes is simply a part of that process. Hopefully, she sees that her teacher is often a student, too.

Christy

I am a great *Googler*. I like to find "the answer." I also hunger and thirst for new ideas, innovative practices, and problem-solving strategies. My favorite aspect of supporting teachers is helping them and watching them, in turn, help their students. But many times, a solution I find or suggest is far from what is needed, is lacking in some feature to accomplish the task, or is completely unusable. Cathy, however, has never once worried or doubted the process. She (as my student at times) allows me (as her teacher at times) the struggle, assists me and lets me learn *with* her. *That* is what collaboration is all about… sharing in the learning with everyone.

Wow! The View from the Penthouse Really IS Worth It!

(The power of reflection and sharing with others)

Cathy

The value of having someone to share with is immeasurable. This piece is really what inspires me to continually challenge myself to keep innovating. Sometimes, just sending a reflection vox (speaking into my phone via Voxer) saying: "Christy, you don't need to answer this, I'm just getting my thoughts out while they're fresh," energizes me to move beyond the present moment…to keep creating, to keep diversifying the instructional strategies for my students' benefit. Knowing someone is sharing my journey, knowing that sometimes my reflections inspire her to support others, makes it even more powerful. I never could have imagined that what happens in an adult ESL classroom in Michigan would be impactful on K12 teachers in Texas!

Christy

I don't think either Cathy or I truly could have predicted the power of the process fueled through connection. So often these days, social media is surrounded by negativity, and the possible positive impact on education is minimized. Neither of us, until we began this writing process, knew just how far we have come *together*, as educators, doing what we love -- *of all ages*! We, ourselves, are lifelong learners and, through what would have been an impossible relationship just a decade ago, we have gained more applicable professional development that translates into the classroom than ever before. This chapter is an integral part of our reflection. We have laughed together (through Voxer and Google Docs chat) about moments forgotten, successes filed in a memory, and the need to revisit some topics again.

Shall We Return to the Lobby? There Are Other Elevator Rides and Views to Explore!

(A look at the future and continuing the conversation)

Cathy

I should note that the connections made with many others on this "elevator ride" of collaboration and connection are influencing my classroom as well. For example, late this past summer, our class "met" online with another educator who was on the Voxer ride - Heidi Carr (@carr_8) from Las Vegas, Nevada. The students prepared a short bio about themselves; they also studied her state of Nevada (using iPads and Google Docs table format for Q&A).

We then "met" Heidi online via Zoom. Though we encountered a little technical difficulty, I was able to help my students virtually experience another location and receive "live" information. The conversation and listening skills used by my students alone was invaluable. I envision our next adventures involving even more collaborative projects with various other technology tools and even options unheard of as of now. We have many tools on our "to try" list! With the class on firm ground with Google Classroom and Seesaw, we are ready to explore more ways to enhance our English fluency.

I would also like to note that our collaboration has begun to extend to my volunteers and other ESL teachers in my region. I have several who pull students out of the class both one-on-one and in small groups. I shared the Google Classroom/Docs table format with one of the more tech-savvy volunteers. He was very excited to see the potential. He took the initiative to explore it, embraced it, and has begun developing his own collaborative lessons with a group that he works with! My other volunteers are less tech-savvy, but are open to learning! I recently had the opportunity to present "How I Use Technology in my ESL Classroom" to a regional adult education workshop!

Christy

As far as I'm concerned, this ride doesn't end. I will continue to celebrate new possibilities with Cathy and her students. I will continue to collaborate with others, test new options, and share with anyone in the classroom environment that wants to grow and brainstorm together. Today's current platforms such as Voxer, Twitter, Google+, LinkedIn, and others make this desire effortless. I can't wait to see the next "view from the top!" Anyone want to join us?

Want to follow along with our learning conversation?		
Elevator Ride	Short Link	QR Code
April 2016 - February 2017	https://goo.gl/npdywH	
March 2017	https://goo.gl/bkTNPw	
April 2017	https://goo.gl/WgVcf4	
Cathy's Presentation on *Using Tech in the Classroom* at an ESL Adult Education Conference	https://goo.gl/iVvRCB	

"Fingers Crossed!"

*We used social media (Facebook Messenger) to send this picture
of everyone with their fingers crossed to Nar K while he was in the
car on his way to his citizenship interview.*

Nar was still studying in the car!

Thanks too everyone!!

A few hours later his daughter-in-law messaged us that he passed! The next day we all celebrated with him!

Nar pass the test

Thanks everyone for your wishes he did it and he is so, happy

Yea!!! Thank you so much for letting us know! We are so happy too!

We are gonna have a little party for him tomorrow!

You are welcome!
He said thanks

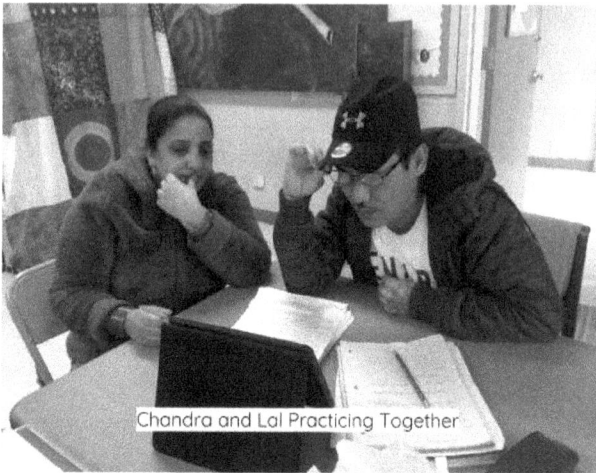

Chandra and Lal Practicing Together

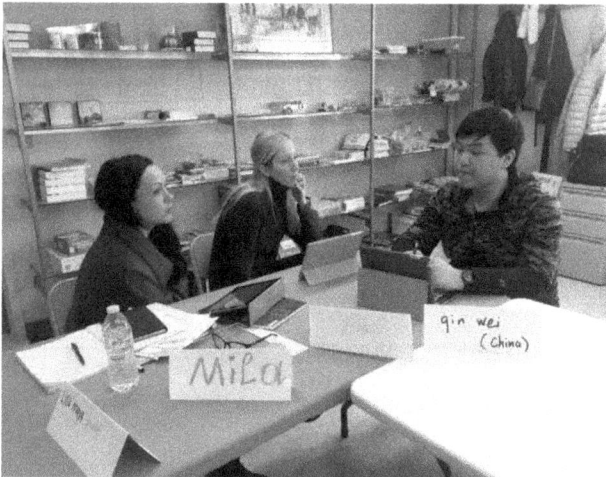

*Mila and Olga from Ukraine practicing conversation with
Qin Wei from China*

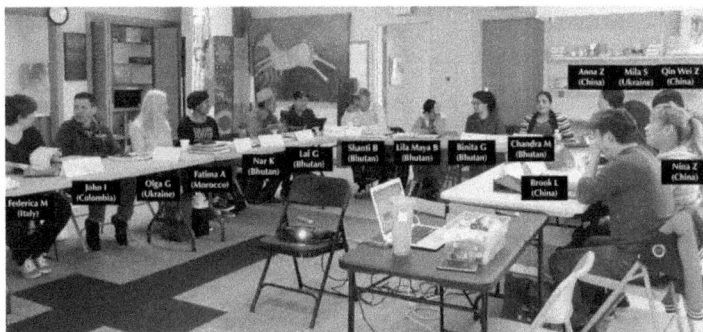

Most of the class practicing conversation together

"Penthouse Views" Videos of Learning in Cathy's Class		
Practicing Colors with Beginning ESL Students Lesson springboard is a Google Doc, colored rods used as manipulatives, students converse and optionally write words on paper. Recorded in Seesaw and published to Seesaw Blog.	https://goo.gl/obYs1R	
CASAS 81-82: What kind of card is this? Shanti B and Lal G learning how to fill out and read a Google Form.	https://goo.gl/Zm4NrR	

CASAS 81-82: What kind of card is this? (Part 2) Shanti B and Lal G learning how to "Submit" and "View Score."	https://goo.gl/gruCqK	
CASAS 81-82: What kind of card is this? (Part 3) Shanti B and Lal G showing how to understand points using rods.	https://goo.gl/uQmBve	
CASAS 81-82: What kind of card is this? (Part 4) Shanti B and Lal G reinforcing the concept of "4 out of 4."	https://goo.gl/adbqRG	

About the Authors

Christy Cate

Christy is Digital Innovation Consultant at Region 14 Education Service Center in Abilene, Texas, serving 42 public school districts. Her current responsibilities involve training and development and evaluation of tools that enhance the classroom experience. Specifically, she is a certified Promethean and SMART trainer, Google Level 1 and Level 2 Certified Educator, Google Certified Trainer, G Suite administrator, Raspberry Pi Certified Educator, LoTi Certified Trainer, and local expert in iOS devices, Web 2.0 tools, and non-traditional instructional strategies.

She has previously served as an educator in both the public and private realms. Her passion for classroom innovation has provided a broad array of content experience, from teaching business, to history, to foreign language, to physical education, to administration. She holds a BA in Human Resource Management and MSE in Counseling from Harding University as well as an M.Ed. in History from Abilene Christian University. Christy has also been privileged to serve on the Board of Directors for TCEA and as organizer for EdCamp West Texas. She is currently the GEG-WESTX Leader. She was honored to be selected as one of "20 to Watch" by the NSBA for 2017. Christy believes in lifelong learning, constant change, and drawing on the expertise of her ever-growing professional learning network. Connect with Christy at @christycate on Twitter, Instagram, Google+, LinkedIn, and Voxer.

Cathy Wolfe

Cathy first began teaching in 1980, then jumped to the business world for 14 years before returning to the classroom. She has a unique instructional experience in that she teaches a multi-level ESL class for adults in Grand Haven, Michigan. Her students include a wide range of ages, cultures, first languages, and educational backgrounds.

She has a passion for supporting students to reach their learning goals, and embraces a flexible teaching style that is open to "whatever works." She also loves technology and is committed to infusing technology into her classes in any way that enhances her students' learning. In December 2015, she stepped onto the ride of expanding her professional learning network by joining Voxer groups mostly populated with K12 educators.

What Was the Spark?

Jason R Falconio

If we don't develop our students as empathetic citizens who can collaborate and care for each other, what have we achieved?

I am writing this chapter a week before we go back to school for the 2017-2018 school year. I am making final preparations to teach my two high school courses, Biology 2 and AP Biology, thinking about what changes I want to make heading into my third year as an Instructional Coach, and preparing for my first year as Science Department Head. I am comfortable saying that I am a pretty good teacher at this point in my career. But, this hasn't always been the case. Early in my career, there was one very bad year, both personally and professionally. I just couldn't get it together in the classroom, and my mother was slowly dying of Early Onset Alzheimer's. My classroom management was rocky at best, I was piecemealing my curriculum, I couldn't focus, and I was behind on many of my duties.

A few days ago, I participated in a writing retreat with an amazing group of educators from Philadelphia, a group that meets regularly to write about educational issues. As we were exploring

some themes in our careers, my colleague Jared
Green asked me what had changed from that
rocky year to the present? I'm clearly in a
different place than I was earlier in my career.

> "What was the spark that
> drove me to become the
> kind of educator I am
> today?"

His question led me to try and distill what
happened early in my career and how that laid the
foundation for what I am about to bring to my
students this coming school year. I have identified
five key things that I did to put my teaching on
the path towards mastery. These five actions were
catalyzed by a workshop I took on *Cooperative
Discipline*[1] by Linda Albert. She delineated the
three C's: to create a cooperative classroom,
students need to feel *capable*, *connect* to each
other, and *contribute* to the class and their
community (Albert, 1996). I have adjusted
Albert's model for my classroom, which contains

---

[1] (n.d.). Cooperative Discipline: Linda Albert:
9780785400424: Amazon.com .... Retrieved October 8,
2017, from https://www.amazon.com/Cooperative-
Discipline-Linda-Albert/dp/0785400427

five C's: *care, capable, collaboration, control,* and *cultural sustainability.* On reflection, I believe that in my own personal and professional growth lay some important lessons for all of us who hope to use the power of education to nurture and support the urban students who are so frequently underserved.

As you sit looking at your lesson plans, what are you stressing about? I'll bet that some form of standardized test looms large in your mind. The pressure we are all under to move students from one level to the next is immense, I know. In my younger years, I would focus on which students I could most likely move from one level to the next and constantly measure my student's academic achievement. Yet, I didn't make as many gains as I thought, and I struggled. Until I decided to put my students' needs first, to care for them, and to find ways to enrich their education, nothing would change. Once I made these shifts and focused on treating my students with respect, understanding their world, and developing their ability to work together, everything changed.

First: I decided to focus on ensuring all students felt cared for in my classroom.

I created a weekly family-style meeting held every Monday in each class. For the first half of the class, each student would share out what was going well for them and what wasn't. Together, we developed norms for our behavior in this space: listening, showing support through words and actions, and celebrating our successes. I have done class meetings every Monday for the past several years, and I can say with confidence, this one step has done more to create a classroom community than anything else I have done. I was initially concerned about giving up 30 minutes, once per week, from my curriculum. What I found was that I didn't lose any time. The trust we built made every other classroom transaction easier.

Another technique I developed was to ensure every interaction was a respectful one. I worked not to yell (I was not always successful here in the early stages). I began to use behavior management techniques from Linda Albert's Cooperative Discipline. These focused on using subtle techniques to teach students how to regulate their own behavior.

The core tenet of this process is my student action plan (Albert, 1996). If a student is doing something that we as a class agreed they should avoid, I might use proximity control to remind the student to adjust and go back to the task at hand. If, after a second reminder, the student continues the behavior, I ask them to fill out a brief action plan. The template asks students to identify their behavior, and then consider whether it fulfilled their needs and what could they do differently next time. The student then leaves the plan on my desk and goes back to work. When I can speak to the student privately, we review the plan and see what I could do to help. This process might take three minutes. It honors the child's voice to determine what they need and how to get it, and it helps keep the class on track.

Second: I worked to find ways to help my students feel they could do the work.

Biology is an extremely challenging topic for any student. My students usually do not have a very strong background in science. There are a lot of reasons for this, but you work with where students are on day one. First, I created learning targets for each unit that students were asked to know. Students were taught each learning target and asked to reflect on their learning of each target. Early on I did this informally, but have developed two methods over the years to formalize this process. First is a portfolio. Each quarter, students submit a series of student work that demonstrates their learning. Students are asked to exhibit how each artifact demonstrated their mastery. Second is a reflection journal. At consistent points throughout the year, students would be asked to reflect on each learning target. I have found the use of the reflection journal to be a little more useful for my class than the portfolio, as it gives students quicker feedback.

If students score under an 80% on any test, they can retake it. I have been teaching long enough that I have a bank of questions to allow me to do this. If students, after reteaching, cannot attain an 80% on the retake, they can complete a mastery project. I've asked students to create their own project, to develop a lesson that they could teach on the topic, or to complete a mastery packet. Each has their benefits, and I use each as I see fit. Each year, in the surveys I give to my students, this opportunity to demonstrate mastery in various ways is the one activity they consistently mention. They often thank me for allowing them to retake assessments. They see that I want them to learn at a pace that works for them, not only what works for me.

I have also created multiple ways for students to show mastery. For each learning target, students usually complete the following: a writing piece, a group POGIL (also known as Process Oriented Guided Inquiry Learning) activity, a modeling assignment, a creative arts assignment (rap, poem, or drawing), and standard multiple-choice and essay assessment. I am working on creating levels for each learning target, almost like a game. Each student can progress through the levels at their own pace. I have done this several times in my genetics unit with great success.

Third: I developed ways for students to collaborate with each other.

We don't have any dedicated lab space at our school, so my classroom doubles as my lab. I usually have about 28-31 students in each class. By the board, I have nine desks in three rows, and around the outskirts of the room, I have six tables that can fit four students each. The combination desk/table layout provides a few benefits. Students that may be distracted or need a little more attention early in the year can sit right up front. Also, some students take time to work well in groups, and the chair layout in the front gives me a chance to help them develop skills to work more effectively in groups. The tables allow me to structure most of my class-time in assignments either done as a pair or in groups of four.

At the start of the year, I spend a lot of time modeling collaboration skills. We watch videos of teams working together and critique them. I build collaboration tasks directly into assignments to help guide them. As needed, in our weekly meetings, we discuss how our collaboration is working and what we can do to improve it. Once we develop a set of skills that will allow students to successfully collaborate, I introduce group tasks (Cohen & Arechevala-Vargas, 1987[2]).

Elizabeth Cohen defines a group task as "a task that requires resources (information, knowledge, heuristic problem-solving strategies, materials, and skills) that no single individual possesses, so that no single individual is likely to

---

[2] (n.d.). 87-3 Interdependence Interaction and Productivity ... - oaktrust.tamu.edu. Retrieved October 8, 2017, from https://oaktrust.library.tamu.edu/bitstream/handle/1969.1/16 1190/%2387-3%20Interdependence%20Interaction%20and%20Productivity.pdf?sequence=1&isAllowed=y

solve the problem or accomplish the task objectives without at least some input from others" (in Cohen & Arechevala-Vargas, 1987). In essence, when doing group work, it can NOT be something the students could complete on their own. Each student needs to bring something unique to the group. This can be in the form of roles. One good reference for using roles is the Process Oriented Guided Inquiry Learning Project, or POGIL[3] (Roles in a POGIL Classroom, 2012).

Also, the task must be guiding students to an ill-structured solution (Cohen, 1994). Ill-structured solutions are problems with more than one way to solve the problem. I might ask students to pretend they are farmers during the dust bowl. Using their knowledge of food webs and energy pyramids, they need to determine how the family can survive the winter. I might ask students to solve how an astronaut can survive on Mars. I might ask students to figure out what the relationship is of two children who are born from two sets of twin parents. I might ask students to

---

[3] (n.d.). POGIL | Roles in a POGIL Classroom. Retrieved October 8, 2017, from http://69.195.198.240/resources/implementation/roles-in-a-pogil-classroom

prove what the evolutionary relationship is between a whale and a hippo. I form a lot of these ill-structured solutions in a case study format.

One excellent resource is the National Center for Case Study Teaching in Science[4]. Case studies are complex enough to require students to gather information, apply it to information they learned in class, and propose a solution, all while making unique contributions to the group.

Another way I focus on collaboration is by using peer tutoring. When students are working to prepare for a summative assessment, I provide them with a set of questions based on the learning targets of each unit. Students who volunteer to become a peer tutor then assist other students in ensuring they understand each learning target and are prepared for the test.

Peer tutors aren't evaluated on the completion of the mastery reflection assignment; they are evaluated on their tutoring ability. I have developed a rubric with my students that evaluates them on skills such as teaching techniques, motivating other students, and professionalism. I also ensure that my peer tutors

---

[4] (n.d.). National Center for Case Study Teaching in .... Retrieved October 8, 2017, from http://sciencecases.lib.buffalo.edu/

aren't just the A students. Any student can be a peer tutor. I have scaffolded supports for peer tutors to help them gain confidence in helping other students. I have slowly worked to increase the use of peer tutoring and teaching because I can see the positive effects it has had on my students: increased attendance, increased grades, increased standardized test scores, and better overall behavior. I have enjoyed using this peer tutoring technique so much, that for the final project in the 2016-2017 school year, my students developed lessons that they will come back this year and teach to my 2017-2018 students. The lessons are robust, creative, and of their choosing; I can't wait to see them in action.

Fourth: I have worked to give students control over my classroom and their learning.

I started working toward this goal a few years ago by adding student jobs to my class. I started with jobs including attendance taker, grade passer-outer, grade collector, and quiz grader. I've done both a rotating assignment and a volunteer system, although I prefer students volunteer for jobs rather than be assigned. I've added a few jobs since then, including the preeminent job of teacher advisor. I meet with the students who are teacher advisors about once a week. We talk about the class and my teaching. We discuss what went well, what didn't, what they like about my teaching, and what they want to change. I got the idea from a talk by Chris Emdin, now fleshed out in his book, *For White Folks Who Teach in the Hood... and the Rest of Y'all Too: Reality Pedagogy and Urban Education*[5]. I've adapted it for use in my classroom.

I've also worked to build time into my curriculum for when the lightbulb goes off within a student, and they offer a suggestion for the class. Most recently, I've begun to move toward a model where students will develop lessons that they will teach the class. It could be on any topic in Biology. Students designed these lessons as a final project (after a suggestion from a few students) and will be co-teaching those lessons with me this calendar year. Some students chose to teach about scientists of their culture, others chose to think about environmental damage to

---

[5] (n.d.). For White Folks Who Teach in the Hood... and the Rest of Y'all Too .... Retrieved September 30, 2017, from https://www.amazon.com/White-Folks-Teach-Hood-Rest/dp/0807006408

urban communities, and some chose to develop lessons on traditional topics in biology.

I love watching students prepare for that next stage in life, where they are in charge of their own choices, which is why I think I teach juniors, those kids on the precipice of adulthood; but in many junior classrooms, especially in urban environments, teachers have consolidated much of the power. Students are expected to do exactly as they are told until they graduate, and then we wonder why they are not prepared for what life throws at them. It was a little scary at first, giving up control of my classroom, but it is worth it. Teenagers need to practice responsibility and ownership. In my classroom, I work to allow them to make choices that affect others and give them time and space to reflect on how that went.

Fifth: I have worked towards developing a culturally sustaining class.

I've made a slow march toward what Django Paris and Samy Alim define as culturally sustaining pedagogy (CSP).[6] They state, "CSP seeks to perpetuate and foster- to sustain- linguistic, literate, and cultural pluralism as part of schooling for positive social transformation. CSP positions dynamic cultural dexterity as a necessary good, and sees the outcome of learning as additive rather than subtractive, as remaining whole rather than framed as broken, as critically enriching strengths rather than replacing deficits" (Paris & Alim, 2017). The stance of enriching strengths speaks to me and my path toward the teacher I am today. As a white teacher, I have worked diligently over the years to develop my thinking about how I can best sustain the cultures of my students, who represent diverse urban communities. I would say the fruition of this thought is coming to bear this coming school year, but I have already laid the groundwork.

Many of my students enjoy hip hop music. At first, I allowed students to substitute a music video for an assignment. I later asked students to help me develop a rubric for such an assignment and then gave them time and space to develop it.

---

[6] (n.d.). Culturally Sustaining Pedagogies 9780807758335 | Teachers College .... Retrieved October 8, 2017, from https://www.tcpress.com/culturally-sustaining-pedagogies-9780807758335

Students submit a rough video which we would review together, and I provide feedback on how their rap or spoken word explains a concept or problem. Students then revise the video and show it to the class. More recently, I've had dedicated assignments integrating parts of their cultural identity such as step shows to demonstrate DNA replication, raps about evolution, and spoken words on genes. I most recently created a set of lessons, which I plan to expand this year, on race and genetics. I used Facing History's Race and Membership[7] resource for help in planning (Race and Membership, 2002). In these lessons, we discuss the biology of race, how society used science to take advantage of certain peoples, and the implications for science today.

A lot has changed in my teaching practice in the last few years. I know I was not in a position as a new teacher to tackle some of these ideas, but now they are foundational in my practice. I now have five key tenets of my practice that I can grow within and beyond this year: caring for my students, ensuring they feel capable, developing

---

[7] (n.d.). Race and Membership in American History: The Eugenics Movement .... Retrieved October 8, 2017, from https://www.facinghistory.org/books-borrowing/race-and-membership-american-history-eugenics-movement

their collaboration, giving them control, and sustaining their culture. I think the lessons I learned speak to the larger issues at work in education. We are under so much pressure to achieve, and we place this on our students. We think testing and measuring them is the answer. I believe, after a decade of teaching, that this is not the answer. If we don't develop our students as empathetic citizens who can collaborate and care for each other, what have we achieved?

Works Cited

Albert, L., Roy, W., & LePage, A. (1989). *A teacher's guide to cooperative discipline: How to manage your classroom and promote self-esteem.* American Guidance Service.

Emdin, C. (2017). *For white folks who teach in the hood ... and the rest of y'all too: Reality pedagogy and urban education.* Beacon Pr.

Paris, D., & Alim, H. S. (2017). *Culturally sustaining pedagogies: Teaching and learning for justice in a changing world.* Teachers College Press.

About the Author

Jason A. Falconio

Jason Falconio has been teaching secondary science for twelve years in both public and charter schools in Philadelphia and Washington D.C. Since 2010 he has been teaching at Freire Charter School in Philadelphia, Pennsylvania. He is currently teaching Biology and AP Biology. Past courses include Physics, Anatomy and Physiology, and General Science. In addition to teaching, he is also an instructional coach and the science department chair. He founded and directed several STEM programs including robotics. In the summer, he works for the Johns Hopkins Center for Talented Youth as a site director. He has his Master's degree in education leadership from Penn State. In 2017, he was named an ASCD Emerging Leader.

Make Believe it is Your First Time

Stephan Hughes

How do you keep the fire of your passion burning?

In a society where individuals are literally summoned to find or to have a passion (who has never been asked, "what's your passion?"), little room has been given to talk about the challenge of keeping the passion alive.

Probably the best way to do that is to do whatever you do as if it were the first time. There is usually something magical, and at the same time petrifying, about a first-time experience; but what moves us is the almost uncontrollable desire to get things right, to meet expectations (ours and of others), to rock the show, to bring the house down, to hit the ball out of the park, to sweep others off their feet. I can go on and on with idioms about causing a good impression.

If we can call up our memory of that first time we did something, we can do that job again and again with nearly the same enthusiasm and gusto from way back then.

Many teachers with at least some years of experience under their belt suffer more from a burning passion than burnout.

How else can we keep the fire of our passions burning?

Practical Tips

1. Listen to the voice in the wilderness - that one student who was not at all blown away by that class everyone said you had aced.
2. Ask yourself if you would like to be in that class.
3. Ask students to critique your lesson plan before the lesson - that means eating huge servings of humble pie.
4. Ask yourself if you would pay to attend your class.
5. ...and don't forget to smile.

About the Author

Stephan Hughes

Stephan has been involved in English Language Teaching for the past 21 years. The move into language learning came with his move to Brazil to learn Portuguese as part of a career goal to become a diplomat. With Spanish and French under his belt at the time, mastering another language would add to his employability, and learning the language spoken in the South American giant poised to take a leadership role on the global stage seemed to be a strategic move.

The country enjoyed a political and economic boom between 2002 and 2014, only to fall into a temporary slump. This has not reduced the need for English language proficiency programs, making it his area of expertise.

Stephan has worked at public and private schools, teaching English as a foreign language to high schoolers. The largest part of his experience has been at a language center that provides English classes to students of all ages, whose goal is to become competent users of the language. Simultaneously, he has delivered lectures as an adjunct professor in a postgraduate program for translators and teachers of English.

In all the diverse professional contexts above, the use of learning technologies and digital resources has been pivotal to delivering high-quality teaching and to foster meaningful learning. Stephan is an aficionado of using whatever technology available that can enhance the learning process, so much so that he often considers himself a self-taught edupreneur.

Choosing Your Battles, Building Relationships and Taking Risks

Fabiana L. Casella

Hold on tight to your dreams

When I was invited by Sarah Thomas to write a chapter for this new edition of the EduMatch Series, I had no words to express the feeling that invaded me! Me writing in English?! Well, yes, let's try! So here I am. I will try to share my deepest feelings and thoughts about my experience as an educator for *thirty years.* Yes, 30 years teaching! I believe I am the eldest in the EduMatch family, but that does not stop me from sharing; quite the opposite, I am now convinced I have to share. Shelly Sanchez Terrell, my mentor, told me once:

"People need to hear your stories and see how you teach. *You have a mission to infect with your enthusiasm.*" She added: "besides, *Presenting and Sharing Your Expertise* is one of the *30 Goals.*[8]"

As a very obedient girl, I followed her advice.

Choosing Your Battles: Maintaining a Peaceful Classroom Environment by Building Relationships

Oh, battles! I've been there so many times! I cannot help it: I teach teenagers, I am an Italian descendant, and I am Argentinian. I was born in the city and have lived in the city all my life...never got used to it, though. We, "City People," battle every single second of our lives:

---

[8] (n.d.). The 30 Goals Challenge. Retrieved November 28, 2017, from http://www.30goals.com/

when we walk, cross the street, commute daily...it is always an adventure with an unknown ending. *It's survival in the city when you live from day to day, city streets don't have much pity, when you're down, that's where you'll stay. (In the City* by Joe Walsh and the Eagles*)*. So, sometimes I feel we are survivors from a tv show. That is why every time I am asked: "How are you doing?" I reply: "I will survive," like Gloria Gaynor.

I mentioned before that I have a saying for every state of mind. There is another response that I have for that "How're you doing?" question, or "¡¿Cómo estás?!" (*How are you?*) To that, I say "Sobreviviendo" (*"Just surviving"*) as Víctor Heredia sings.

Inspired by another song, this time one from a local musician, wonderful composer, and lyricist. Some may think he talks about a certain time in Argentine history, but I take the song as my personal "anthem": it is all about choosing peace, not war; life, not death; good, not bad; love, not hate.

However, our battles inside a class are different, at least for me, because I have taught teenagers since 1988, and generations have evolved so much since then. Nowadays, adolescents are not the same as adolescents in the nineties, or at the beginning of this century. Since

I started teaching back in Argentina, my home country, I have been working hard on my professional development. I have discovered a wonderful author named Michael Linsin, whose blog, "Smart Classroom Management,[9]" and book, *Dream Class*[10], have made me rethink what I am doing inside the class. I began to consider a future project where I could give advice about classroom management to new teachers, and to veteran teachers, who sometimes need to recharge batteries and add some oil to their engines. (I have been watching Pixar's Cars a lot lately!)

In his article, "Why Picking Your Battles Is a Poor Strategy,[11]" Linsin says that picking your battles only causes more misbehavior, resentment and although it might work with some "difficult" students and/or classes, it will prevent us from

─────────────────────

[9] (n.d.). Smart Classroom Management. Retrieved November 28, 2017, from https://www.smartclassroommanagement.com/
[10] (n.d.). Dream Class: How To Transform Any Group Of ... - Amazon.com. Retrieved November 28, 2017, from https://www.amazon.com/Dream-Class-Transform-Students-Always/dp/1889236330
[11] (2013, June 8). Why Picking Your Battles Is A Poor Strategy - Smart Classroom .... Retrieved November 28, 2017, from https://www.smartclassroommanagement.com/2013/06/08/why-picking-your-battles-is-a-poor-strategy/

creating the well-behaved classroom we really want. On the contrary, picking your battles can:

- cause resentment.
- cause teachers to lose trust.
- be confrontational.
- encourage arguing.
- cause disrespect.
- be unnerving to students (my favorite one).

Linsin writes:

> How does one go about picking battles? Is it based on the severity of the misbehavior, who is doing the misbehaving, the teacher's mood at the time? The truth is, leaving classroom management so haphazardly defined causes tension and anxiety and creates a climate students don't want to be part of.

Teaching in Argentina has become a little more complicated than when I was in my 30s

because our society has undergone many (I would
say *too* many) severe crises, both economic and
psychological. The ones who suffer the most are
the children, and at our school, we try to turn
misbehaved students and "warriors" into good
soldiers, ready to battle life outside the nice, cozy
and comfortable school environment.

I cannot stop thinking of those sad events at
Sandy Hook, or even here, in a small town called
Carmen de Patagones. Unfortunately, *violence
asks for violence*; peace brings peace. Do not give
way to "battles" in our classrooms, let us free
them from the stress and wasted time. Do some
"system restore," run that annoying update, and
bring back peace and restoration to our favorite
place: our class. Stick to your classroom
management plan. I am talking about well-taught
and consistent classroom rules. Seek help from a
colleague. Ask him to watch your class.
Encourage positivism in students, and bear in
mind that sometimes peace is better than being
right.

Taking Risks: Adversity and Obstacles Made Me a More Resourceful Teacher

Back in the late 1980s, I started teaching English as a Foreign Language at a primary school, and at a private language school for children, teens, and adults. The only materials we had were a course book, workbook, and cassettes to practice listening comprehension. We also watched films for listening and speaking practice. The tapes would stop working in the tape player from time to time because they had been used too many times. Rewinding and fast forwarding to find the right lesson made them unplayable in a short time.

Times changed, so we started to use CDs, and later USB **flash drives,** or **pen drives**, as they are called here in Argentina. (I really have not found what the difference between the two words is).

My *first close encounter* with technology was when I began to teach in the US in 2001. I had an Apple computer in the classroom, free access to many computers in the school library, and laptops in a cart that I could book in advance. I could take the laptops to my classroom so that my students could surf the web and see what we Argentinians actually look like. It was like a dream! The fact that I could email anyone, at any time really helped me adapt to being away from my relatives and friends in my home country. I was teaching in a completely different environment from the one I was used to. I was not only *amazed* by the use of technology in the classes, but also by the organization and simplification of school life in many aspects.

Did all this advancement require training or rehearsing before each class when I wanted to implement some of this revolutionary technological practice? It was a question of self-motivation, curiosity, and self-assessment. I would sit at my desktop computer and start playing with the different tools to make, for example, my own school webpage.

I included background tango music, filled with Argentine websites, maps, places to visit, and also homework, classwork, extra practice, and much more. It goes without saying that anything related to technology was not such a big surprise to my students, as it was for me. Through SchoolNotes, the District provided every teacher the possibility to have her/his own webpage! Amazing! I added all I could...tango music in the background, links to Argentinian websites in Spanish and English, alongside the day's activities, weekly planning, and homework.

In those years, my professional development happened almost accidentally every single day. The moment I landed in my former classroom in Argentina in 2010, the feeling of frustration and disappointment began growing again. It was not the school environment or unresponsive students; quite the opposite. Students, or at least those who had internet on their personal phones, were fascinated to Tweet about World Peace Day prepare lessons on segregation in the US, celebrate World Water Day, or criticize the United Nations. They had a voice in my classes: I hadunconsciously started the #studentvoice trend.

As I stayed in touch with my former colleagues in the US, I became aware that technology and global connections were being implemented very seriously in the classrooms. I had experienced that myself: my ESOL students were using Google Earth to locate their hometowns, practicing pronunciation, and studying Math, Science and Social Studies online. In 2011 in Argentina, Blackberry cellphones were already on the market. Impressed, we would say, "Wow!! You have a Blackberry!"

After seeing how many of my students had a smartphone, I felt I had to do something new, innovative, and creative. I could not sit still, waiting for digital devices to be delivered to my classroom. I had to look for a way to work with those phones that my students had, although I did not have one myself. ***I NEEDED to innovate***! I had to! I could not accept I was in a classroom environment where books, CDs, and paper handouts were the only resources available. Soon, I decided to buy an LG cell phone with a built-in camera to take photos and record video: two GB but not able to connect to the Internet. So, I started taking pictures and recording very bad quality videos of my students' projects.

Later that same year, I enrolled in an online course offered by one of the most well-known technological universities and delivered by a very well-known specialist. My *innovative educator life* began at the same moment that I was invited to join the 30 Goals Challenge for Educators.

Why did I mention *adversity* and *obstacles* if all I had written here were mainly successful events?

All that glitters is not gold, oh yes! I had to face adversity, and tackle or kick obstacles out of my way. Power outages, exams rescheduled, health problems, not being recognized for my teaching background and knowledge, low pay and low budgets. They were enough reasons to quit...obstacles and more obstacles...but my self-motivation and faith helped me see the light at the end of the dark tunnel.

As most of the things that happened to me (and the people around me), doing our daily routines without knowing if we were going to have power for 24 hours or less was **awfully** stressing. It was not awful to think of the answers, what was **horrible** was to be **so engaged and willing to work, think of every answer to the wonderful interview,** but not in such terrible conditions. Honestly, I was anxiously waiting for December to come, to be able to sit down and work on the interview. How naive I was! We had the worst end of year I remember in all my life: every day was a nightmare, an empty fridge, no fans, no AC, no nothing. Nights were hot as h***. Why? Any answers? Sure! Just read below.

Those who do not know me well may think I am determined to be a teaching star, or become famous by talking about what I do or what I do not do in my classes. There are hundreds of teachers out there doing what I do in a much better way. My friends from Argentina have been teaching wonderfully and super creatively for years and never showed anything to anyone.

Sharing what I do and who I am really lifts me up. I have always been open to sharing and learning. Maybe that is why I chose this profession. Maybe that is why I am where I am: blogging, studying online, posting on Twitter, Facebook, and chatting on Voxer…exchanging thoughts and ideas with all my friends and colleagues…growing as a connected educator, participating in debates, and presenting for the first time in my life. All of these things have helped me to overcome a huge personal crisis: frustration over being back home.

Being back home meant happiness to see relatives and friends anytime we wanted, because we only visited them once a year in June and July. Being back home meant getting used to doing things we had done before, but it also meant living in a way that was not very satisfying. We left behind the peace and quiet of living in the delightfully peaceful city of Salisbury, Rowan County, North Carolina.

In the beginning, adjusting to life in a foreign country was not easy at all, but once we got most of our things set up, it was total relaxation. As for me, as an exchange teacher, **every single school day was a day of training.** In addition to teaching and adjusting to classroom rules and school rules, I interacted with so many colleagues: administrators, staff, attendance monitors, guidance counselors, athletic coaches, the school's deputy, cafeteria staff, and Hazel, the sweet lady who cleaned our classroom. I even spoke with the police officer! *All of them* became **part of my daily professional development.**

Leaving frustration behind...what a challenge, oh Lord! No matter what, I tried to hold on tight to my dreams...

Those dreams were to build a class full of learning, entertainment, knowledge sharing, teamwork, motivation, behavior, achievement, leaving stress aside. Those dreams required me to take risks and try new ways to transform the traditional way English as a Foreign Language classes had been taught. Why did I take those risks? Why *do I talk about risks?* I risked it all for my students. They deserved it. I did face challenges and criticism, although all my intentions were the best I could offer my students and their families, to whom I dedicate my passion and hard work.

I would like to explain to those that are taking the time to read this, that I am talking about two different types of risks: *the ones I take in class and the ones I take after class.*

"Mystery Skype" was *my* goal and biggest risk in 2015. If I could connect my students with a class in another country, they would never forget the experience of speaking in English, live and with real people. I soon realized that the real risk was to Mystery Skype without a reliable Internet connection and sound. There were problems with the bandwidth, and I spent two classes trying to connect. The first time, we had video and sound;

the second time, we had sound, but no video. We
are all vulnerable as educators, and we have to
solve problems the moment they are present. The
main concern around my school was why the
students were so loud and laughing so much.
Later, people understood: students were having
fun sharing hints and clues about our school, our
city, and country in order to be "discovered!" I
am convinced that things happen for a reason.
There are those moments that wake you up.

> "Haters will hate," Nikki
> D Robertson said during
> her keynote for the 30
> Goals WebConference.

That quote has resonated in my mind since I
listened to it and that is when I renewed my
strength and got ready to fight the upcoming
battles. Soon after that, I found encouragement
and more motivation from tweets, talks and links
to blog posts written by another EduGuru, Eric
Sheninger's "Take Risks, Learn, Model.[12]" He
talks about schools in general, and how they are

---

[12] (2013, December 8). Eric Sheninger: Leadership 2.0 -
YouTube. Retrieved November 28, 2017, from
https://www.youtube.com/watch?v=kirJZVGWOcE

not being shaped to satisfy students´ abilities and capabilities. Even his own children hate school, and that really spoke to me because my daughter who is almost ten now, became tired of school when she was only in second grade.

I will probably write about this issue in the following edition...

#GlobalAmbassador

About the Author

Fabiana L. Casella

Fabiana Casella is a passionate EFL teacher, an Education and ICT Specialist, Microsoft Certified Innovative Educator Expert, Trainer, and Guest Speaker from Argentina. Since 1989, Fabiana has been teaching secondary school, and tutoring children and adults at language schools. She taught ESL and Spanish at the high school and middle school levels in the United States. She was awarded the Cultural Exchange Ambassador Diploma by Visiting International Faculty, now Participate, in North Carolina. Being a Cultural Exchange Educator, getting involved in social media education sites, applying tech tools in her classes, staying in touch and participating in projects with educators around the world, blogging and presenting online has had a tremendous impact on her teaching life.

Fabiana is a blogger at British Council Teaching English, a member of the Argentinian Teacher's Association A.P.I.B.A., IATEFL, #EdSpeakers and iTDi mentor. In 2015, she was selected to participate at iEARN Brasilia, and she won a scholarship on Academic Writing from APIBA/FAAPI (Argentina). In 2016, she was named Buncee Ambassador, and she was recently appointed Global Peer Reviewer Mentor for Participate.

fabianacasella@gmail.com
Facebook: Fabiana Casella
Twitter: @FabLCasellaEdu
Skype: fabianna.casella
Blogger: http://all4efl.blogspot.com.ar/
Website:
fabianacasella.wixsite.com/globaleducator

Perseverance

Heidi Carr

Do not hold anyone back from collecting their pearls.

"Mr. Jones asked me the other day, 'Didn't Heidi struggle in reading and need to go to Mrs. Smith's class for assistance?'" Ms. Johnson said.

My heart sank, as this is how Mr. Jones remembered me. He had told other teachers this when he heard I wanted to student teach with Ms. Johnson. No matter my age or accomplishments, in their eyes, I was labeled as the "struggling reader!"

I cried and cried, and thought there is no way I could successfully complete my student teaching with Ms. Johnson and the other teachers, because in their minds they did not see me as capable of teaching. I questioned myself and wondered many times if I could do this. I almost talked myself out of becoming a teacher, but my mom and dad believed in me and reminded me that I would be a fabulous educator because I had overcome many obstacles in life. "Do not let others steer you away from your dreams, Heidi Carr," they told me.

That really is my dream! Ever since third grade, I have wanted to be a teacher. I used to have this blue bag in which I saved all my school stuff and would play school with the neighborhood kids. Danielle and I would always be the teachers. One reason I think I wanted to become a teacher was because of a handwritten note on my fraction homework one day. In bright RED pen, "Mr. Carr, please do not ever help Heidi with her homework again." I was devastated because I did not understand fractions, but was able to understand my dad's strategies. Yes, my answers were correct; however, we did not solve them HER way.

My determination then is what continues my drive now. Yes, I fail, but my mistakes do NOT define what I am capable of. Learning from our mistakes is powerful! I have a mission to instill this principle into the hearts and minds of each child in my classroom

In my "Carrific" class, we allow students to make and share mistakes, along with successes. This is how we learn and grow together. Many educators tell their students daily to persevere, but do they model it? Are you an educator who attaches labels to students? If José or Heather were "labeled" as a bad kid, do you see him or her as "bad?" If so, why?

I challenge you to take that label off and allow the students to show you who they really are! Allow their inner lights to shine! Without some of my teachers who avoided labeling me, had high expectations and challenged me to reach for the stars, I still could have been "that student" who never improved in reading.

Yes, it takes a village to raise a child, and without teachers and parents who encouraged me to persevere, I would not be where and who I am today.

I remember when I ran into that particular group of teachers from my hometown, and they asked how I was doing. I was extremely proud to say, "I am a teacher!" The look on Mr. Jones's face and on the faces of the others was priceless! They asked a few questions which led me to tell them some of my accomplishments, of which one of them was receiving my Master's degree from the University of Nevada - Las Vegas (UNLV).

After I walked away, I felt invigorated, vindicated, and encouraged because I did not let the stigma of being a struggling reader growing up define me. I refuse to say I beat the odds, because I truly believe that with perseverance and determination *anything* is possible! How will you make sure you inspire and nourish all your students to reach their fullest potential? You might be that *one* person who pushes them just enough to set them on a path on which they never knew they could go.

I'm thankful that my support system allowed me to make mistakes, but continued to challenge me to be more. Our students deserve the opportunity to reach for their dreams. It is, therefore, important to truly listen to them. And remember: what we say to our students *does* resonate in young, impressionable minds. Choose your words carefully and with purpose. When students have perseverance and dedication, the world is their oyster. Do not hold anyone back from collecting their pearls.

* All names have been changed to protect privacy.

About the Author

Heidi Carr

Heidi Carr is an elementary facilitator and educational leader that strives to provide professional example to other educators, parents, and the community. She is the current President of CUE-Nevada, and founded the NVEdu Voxer group and Playdate Vegas.

Heidi is an innovator, risk-taker, and is always willing to go the extra mile to meet her students' needs. She believes that all students should have their own individualized plan, and is an advocate for all students. She especially has a passion working with inner-city children. Heidi has collaborated with Nevada State College and Las Vegas Housing Authority where she ran after-school and summer programs in Sherman

Gardens and Ernie Cragin Public Housing Complexes.

She grew up in Northern Nevada and graduated with a Bachelor's in Elementary Education from Nevada State College and a Master's in Curriculum and Instruction from University Las Vegas Nevada.

Connect with Heidi at @carr_8 on Twitter and Voxer or on Google+.

IF THE SHOE FITS

Barbara Cotter

A global educator's journey of perseverance for transformative professional growth in a global education race

Finding the Right Shoes

You know that old saying, "walk a mile in my shoes..." Well, you know the rest. Whoever said this probably had not experienced a good jog, or a walk either. That's my assumption at least.

Believe me, as an educator, you not only walk or jog, but in many instances, have to run with a great idea that you would like set in motion. It's what makes the best of educators tick. Educators are to be flexible, agile, witty, current, tech-savvy, patient, insightful, brilliant, considerate, frugal, counselors, loyal, fanny-smoochers, psychics, naturalists, realists (and the list can be most daunting, oh, and exhaustive). Did I miss anything?

I know, describing the plethora of roles that are designated to educators makes you wonder why many of the loyal ones haven't run the "Education Marathon." Or have they co-chaired many already? Maybe it's because we are having a hard time trying to catch up to some of them. It feels like a rabbit chasing a carrot on a stick, right?

Having to keep up with all that is *education* is a shoe that many educators, novice or expert, have quite the task of fitting. The world of learning is our "Global Foot Locker." We as devoted educators have a task, to not only find the shoe that fits right, but also knowing beforehand, the purpose these shoes ought to serve. A bad fit is a mishap in the making.

So much is at stake when it comes to making a judgment call, where learning is concerned. You not only think from the end recipient's point of view, but also yours. (Yes, you do have to consider yours as an educator.) After all, you will be the one orchestrating the walk, jog, or run. Yes, *you* will be orchestrating the Education Marathon.

Irrespective of where you are as an educator, professionally and personally, knowing your limits is critical to determining your psyche for this long haul. Sometimes the shoes fit perfectly, until you realize that they won't work for any-and-every terrain or circumstance. Having to be quick in making last-minute adjustments seems like you've now also undertaken the role of cobbler.

Yes, I know: one more to add to your title. But isn't that why we as educators are sometimes mistaken for "fairy godparents?" Yes, we have to "think on our feet" (literally), as any other stance would be considered lackadaisical.

To the eyes of the onlookers, since when are educators known to "sleep?" Do we really do that? Or, is that all taboo? Walking a mile in an educator's shoes is no easy feat (pun intended). Knowing where to begin as far as finding the right task, the right resources, the right stakeholder pitch, the right proposal, the right *time*...all too critical in making the best or most suitable judgment call.

No educator wants to commence an academic year with mismatched shoes or decisions. It makes for a very rocky start. So how we as educators choose to commence this journey, this walk, this jog, this run, heck *this educational marathon*, is certainly dependent on preparation. Finding the right shoe, befitting the long journey up ahead.

Going the Distance

So, we are off to what we deem a "good" start. I hesitate to use the word "great" for fear of having to jinx it. After all, lots of preparation has gone into play to ensure getting us off on the right footing (yes, pun intended again).

Now that we have found the right shoes for the journey ahead, we now focus on psyche for going the extra mile. Yes, the extra mile is what will set us apart. Being an educator who stands out from among the rest, irrespective of your pains from not "warming up" properly before the race, is of no concern to the onlookers.

No, it's not just about impressions or your ego anymore. It's all about how far you as a determined, goal-oriented, transformative mindset, get-your-feet-wet educator you are.

Are you willing to "go the distance?" That "distance" need not be solely a spatial one. That distance is what truly sets the dedicated educator apart from the rest of the crowd. You know exactly what I'm talking about…that wonderful thing called "Professional Growth."

Many dread it and regard it as this one more hurdle to go over, a possible ankle weight to "supposedly" strengthen our psyche, in preparation for amazing learning. How far are you willing to push yourself emotionally and psychologically?

Yes, we all have our limits, but sometimes we don't even know when we've reached them or just how much further we can truly go. That, to me, is not a risk, but rather an opportunity for growth.

That growth is not only noticeable from within one's self, but rather from the actions exemplified and manifested to those we encounter. The most influential spectators are our learners…yes, the ones we certainly are desirous of impacting. The ones who might, someday, be future educators themselves. The very ones who motivate us to do venture on different paths, and in varied directions, even when we know fully well that we will yet arrive at our desired destination.

We aren't going the extra mile, really. We are just strategizing. We need to focus on what "we" the learners and educators (which, by the way, are interchangeable), will need to accomplish to make the journey seem less mundane.

I used to own a shirt back in the 80's that said, "Same S#!t, Different Day," and really felt that way because I never allowed myself to take control. Simply taking control of whatever outcome you'd like to attain doesn't make you a Pilot educator. This is taking control in the sense that you feel adequately prepared, because you have more back-ups in your backpack than your neighborhood power company.

You've seen many of your colleagues fall along the wayside for that very lack of preparation and level of control. One slip up, and it's "bye, bye, baby."

The control you exercise is also within yourself, knowing exactly how tight to hold on and when to let go. Letting go, by the way, is the masterful demonstration of your control tactics.

Yes, it's fairly easy to tell yourself as an educator that "[you've] got this." Now, telling yourself as an educator going the distance that your learners "got it" too is the refreshing feel of the water being splashed on your face as you continue to pace yourself. The transformation of the mind is beginning to take shape. Once the mind becomes a receptacle to allowing that change, the body willingly engages and moves effortlessly and with little resistance.

Along the Way

So, the mindset is no longer a "mindset" but rather a "transmind," a mind in transition and transformation as you pace yourself through the academic marathon/relay. Now it may seem like an eternity, but once you're all geared up appropriately, you'll slowly but surely gain much momentum.

This transformation can turn out to be a
marathon for you (if you so choose), or a relay.
This again goes back to the control you are
desirous of relinquishing or keeping a tight rein
on. Think of those tight reins as your sweatband
(if they still exist). You know, that thing you wear
around your head to prevent the sweat from
getting into your eyes. Ok, so I've brought you
back to the 20th century.

Those sweatbands aren't just an athletic
accessory. They do, in fact, serve a purpose. They
help to capture the sweat that trickles down from
your head, to prevent them getting into your eyes.
Without them, you'd be constantly flicking sweat
from your face with your hands. That action alone
changes the pace of your strides and certainly
your momentum. Get the sweatband.

Yes, those things that seem unnecessary at
first glance in your educational community might
actually benefit your growth, once you allow
them to be absorbed mentally, and even
emotionally, into your educator veins…those
wonderful things called webinars, conferences,
edcamps, breakout sessions, Twitter chats, vlogs,
and blogs. The list is endless.

All of these professional outlets along the
way aren't meant as hurdles or curves on the
course. They are the very elements that
necessitate your existence as a "professional," as a

true "transformative educator." You may think you are going to this event as an individual, but, in fact, you have your entire team and sponsors all rooting for you.

And yes, there are even paramedics there, too.

What may seem like an eternity as you continue on this race is again dependent on your "transmind," how receptive or repelling you are to ideas, collaboration, and connecting with many in the same shoes as yourself. Look around you. No one runs a race and hopes to win when they are running alone. Your support system will always be ready and waiting, should you beckon them. There has never been an "I" in TEAM, and for a good purpose, too, because together with your PLS (Professional Learning System), the event seems a lot less daunting. Less mundane. Less painful. Less disheartening. Your supportive and go-to PLS are ready to provide the aid you need, when you need it. All you need do is A.S.K. (ALWAYS SEEK KNOWLEDGE).

Your faithful colleagues and PLS have always been there to either take the baton in the professional relay, or to bellow on the megaphone should they see the need to uplift you. As a put-together professional educator, you are *never* alone. You may think at times to quit before you pull a hamstring. Again, remember that should you be so lucky (grin), your paramedic PLS are there for you. Many have run the same events as you, and know too well how it feels to give it your all, not just for your growth, but for the growth of your learners…your onlookers. Just keep moving, just keep moving.

Possible End in Sight

You've gained confidence, momentum, and poise. It shows all over your smirking face and in your strides. They have become calculated at times, and yet unpredictably anticipated. Your learners look forward to all that you have to offer because they, too, felt very much included in your preparation.

Nonetheless, let not your guard down, for all it takes is a moment of hesitation…a split-second glance away from your goal and target. Stay focused always. Remember, there are others of like mind, running with you.

You are tempted to look back to see the competition. But I tell you, moving *forward* is far more fun when your face is fixated on your frivolous fans cheering you on near the finish line. They are the reason for your participation in this event. They are the reason you went the extra mile gearing yourself up like never before. They are the reason for you being in the best professional shape of your career.

You begin to realize what being a "True Transformative Educator" is all about. The changes become more and more apparent in yourself, and from their expressions, theirs as well. Those days and nights when all you wanted to do was head straight to your room and lock yourself away from everyone else, is becoming a thing of the past.

You recognize now that the greatest of many like you have fallen to the same thought, but what makes them ever the greatest is their desire to pick themselves up and try again. Your clenched jaw shows your learners and onlookers your humanity. It shows them the pain and exasperation you feel going through this. It then becomes a learning experience, not only for you but for them alike. They now see what persistence and dedication look like. You no longer become an eidolon to them. To them, you are authentic.

This authenticity is sometimes so lacking in the education system that you begin to wonder what is real and what is a mirage. Your training and preparations that have led up to this day, and nearing the end now has affirmed your true purpose: your true transformative self.

You've engaged beyond the learning environment. You've allowed yourself to try something new, something different, something outside of your realm of possibilities. What's more, you've gone out and tried on someone else's shoes to gain a varying perspective on things.

Sure, you had to try on many before finding the best fit, but look at you now. The extra time taken to undergo the preparations is beginning to pay off. You feel so much more confident. Nothing thrown at you will frazzle you. Your PLS is not a joke. They are truly the best thing since spandex, and you know it. You quickly realize that you're nearing the finish line and it suddenly hits you.

"Do I even want this to end?"

"Do I want to disrobe myself?"

"I'm really digging those sneakers now."

Those sessions, conferences, edcamps, webinars, breakout sessions, expos, Twitter chats, blogs, vlogs, Flipgrid, Voxer groups, and the too numerous PDs you once dreaded have transformed you, all for the better...all for your growth and that of your onlookers and spectators. Your fans are so grateful for the "New You." You love how you now feel, and what you feel you can truly accomplish as you propel yourself to the finish line. But does it have to really end there?

The Finish Line...?

You're nearing the finish line and thinking to yourself, "I've got this one in the bag." You're not looking behind you anymore. It's behind you for a reason. You can't propel yourself to greatness if you keep looking back. Every turn in the opposite direction is a dawdle of doom. Keep moving forward.

You may be nearing what seems to be the finish line, but it doesn't have to come to a screeching halt there. Use those great ideas, new techniques, new practices, and new resources in not just the ways they may have been intended, but in a way that works for you and your learning community. Always be willing to be in a transformative state of mind and doing. Those shoes will wear out, that headband will be dated, that spandex...well, we'll keep the spandex.

Those onlookers will change (as will you), but all for the better. You've gone beyond walking a mile in someone else's shoes. You've run the educational marathon/relay, and by golly, it feels great. You've persevered. You've gained a new "transmind" on all possibilities and what seemed daunting at first, now seems doable. It feels *great*.

You may have come to the climax of an academic year, but you know it to be your anti-climax of many still to come.

You're ecstatic about nearing the end, but not with the intention to just complete the race. Rather you're piqued by having to do this all again for the upcoming year. Nothing, and no one, can stop you now. You now know of aches and pains where you didn't feel it would be possible to feel that much agony. You now know what it means to have a great support system that has your back, and you, theirs.

You now know of proper preparation for all things that may come your way...the jeers, the stares, the "bewares" that have been most evident. You know of control, when to relinquish and when to hold tightly to the reins. You now know how to adjust your pace with your team in mind. You now know that no two shoes are alike, that not all shoes will fit all circumstances and events. You now know to embrace change that would allow you to be a better you for yourself, and for others. You now know where to go, should you come across a hurdle or obstacle. You now know what it means to be a persistent educator who embraces change in a transformative way, through perseverance and dedication.

This race or this event may have initially been on a regional level, but now you've gotten your feet wet for nationals, and yes, even international exposure. The terrain, the setting, the time and place may differ, but all that has led to you being a part of it is no different. You don't want to just walk a mile in someone else's shoes. You are ready to run with theirs, and yes, even your own. Your shoes fit just fine, but you know what it takes to try on different shoes. You know exactly what it feels like to stumble along the way and get back in the game. It may seem like you've come to the finish line, but to you, as a transformative professional educator, with a "transmind," you will keep moving forward and keep on propelling yourself. The end is never the end.

The Medal Podium

The fanfare and celebrations are in order. The festivities commence for a job well done. Who doesn't welcome medals and trophies under their belts? They are far more than extrinsic for those who partake for a purpose beyond the medal count. They are pleasant reminders of the progress we make as we continue to grow as professionals. They are representations of our struggles, successes, efforts, and certainly hard work. Sure, we don't do it all for the glamour. But sometimes a boost is greater than a bust. We all seek to be on the podium at some point in our professional journey. That's what makes opportunities for other great races and events all the more possible. Running those educational marathons/relays in our neck of the woods is great. But, oh, the sense of purpose, accomplishment, and the chance to try new things will only be within grasp when others know of our great strides.

Enjoy the spotlight when you can. If you're not in it, try moving yourself to another mark. Maybe you just missed it by a hair. That's why you, as an educator, are to be so agile, so open, so willing to move and venture into new areas.

The medal podium is not a finite space. There's always plenty of room up there for those willing to try something different or something new. There always an award that hasn't been handed out yet. There's always room for success. It's there waiting for you to try on. Adjust where necessary. Just know that in the educational marathon/relay, we were all winners the moment we decided to join the race.

About the Author

Barbara Cotter

Barbara Cotter is a Technology Integration Specialist, Computer Educator, Curriculum Developer, Technology Director, independent educational consultant, and Coordinator with 28 years of experience for grades PreK-Adult. She has been privileged to have acquired this experience in the USA, as well as internationally. She regards herself as a transformative agent of change with connections globally, and a continuously evolving mindset. Barbara is a lover of all things tech, STEM, and coding, both in and out of the learning environment, yet balanced with a passion for the great outdoors. Her motto is "be the change you want to see."

Post-Concussion

Stephanie Filardo

What a car accident taught me about my students

When I found out I had a concussion, I didn't think it would impact my life in the way it did. Honestly, I felt fine -- for about 12 hours. Then the way I look and interact with everything in my life changed. About a week in, I knew I wanted to remember and catalog this journey, but I wasn't able to. I dictated thoughts on my phone, but it just wasn't what I was used to doing. It's hard for me to listen to myself be so -- *vulnerable*, and for this reason, this writing will be the least edited I've put out to the world. I am fortunate my injuries weren't worse, but I'm still healing. And, as I've learned, healing is a process, especially for the impatient ones like me.

I share this for many reasons, but mostly for me. I don't want to forget what I went through, what I am going through. At the very least, I don't want to forget that I was able to better understand some of my students' struggles.

POST-CONCUSSION:
WHAT A CAR ACCIDENT
taught me about my students

Stephanie Filardo - @i3algebra - i3algebra.blogspot.com

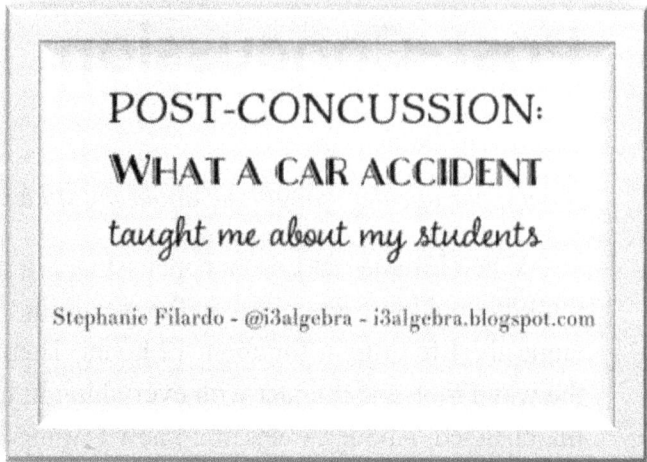

December 27th

I was leaving my sister's house, driving along the gravel road, when the loose gravel carried me into a tree lining the side of the road. I wasn't going very fast, but in a matter of seconds, my car was totaled. I wasn't looking at my phone, distracted. Something had caught my attention, and I looked in the rearview mirror for a moment too long.

My first collected moment was hearing my phone ringing. Remembering I had set up 911 assist, I tried to end the call. I was fine. Sure, my car was not in good shape, and in the middle of the road, but I was fine. My nose hurt a bit from the force of the airbags punching me at full force, and there was this burning sensation. I guess airbags are basically fireworks inside your car.

I couldn't figure out how to end the call. My car wouldn't let me.

I was sitting in the middle of the road, sideways. The last thing I remembered after the airbags going off was looking forward, yet seeing down the hill. I closed my eyes and braced for the trip over the edge. Now I was in the middle of the road, turned 90 degrees from where I'd been before.

I tried to call my sister. She didn't answer. I thought, *maybe I should run to her*, then a car came along and stopped to help. They couldn't really go any further since the road was completely blocked. My right shin hurt. Stupid knee airbags...more like ankle airbags for me. I knew this would hurt tomorrow.

I got a good look at my car. It was toast. My ears were ringing, and I wasn't sure how much time had passed.

The view from my sister's car while we waited for the tow truck.

The EMTs cleared me but told me I should see my doctor anyway. I passed all of the neurological tests they gave me. I remember them saying my vitals were "something to be admired." Maybe it's a teacher thing, calm during the storm and all. I went home to sleep. I just wanted the day to be over.

December 28th

The pain, I expected, but the nausea started just before I called my doctor to schedule a visit. A trip to urgent care it is!

My ears are still ringing…I'm not sure I should be alone, let alone drive. A friend drives me to urgent care. I'm told that I pass all the neurological tests again, but I still don't feel right. The diagnosis is a concussion. My students have had these, many on more than one occasion, but my airbags went off. I wasn't driving very fast. It just doesn't make sense to me. I'm supposed to go home and rest. At least I'm still on break.

December 29th

After being cooped up in the house for longer than I'm used to, I go out to eat. It's hard to hear everyone's conversations and focus on the one I'm supposed to be having, but I really don't think much of it...that is, until I'm at the counter, paying my bill. I'm trying to add 27+5, and I can't do it. *I can't hold focus on the task at hand no matter how hard I try. I hear every conversation, clear as day and muffled at the same time. Dishes are clanging on the buffet line. Sizzling at the hibachi station. Children tapping their cups with forks. People eating. Lights buzzing. I could hear everything, and I couldn't block any of it out.* Determined, I focus on my hands. "27" I point at one of my fingers: "28," another, "29," another "30," until I have 5 fingers up. I may not teach math this year, but I'm a math teacher. This isn't happening to me. I sign the receipt and nearly burst into tears as I walk out of the restaurant. My brain is broken, and I'm locked inside.

This isn't right. None of this is right. I end up in the emergency room later that night because, either my concussion made me so nauseous I threw up, or the thought of me not being me was much more than I could handle. I still don't know.

NOTE: I've been through simulation activities for ADHD and specific learning disabilities. I wouldn't wish this restaurant experience on anyone, but if I could have others experience it, I would. Maybe they would understand what many of our students go through in our classrooms.

December 30th

Brain rest is boring. Nothing with a screen, no reading, no thinking. Brain rest is boring.

Note: I didn't even write this part that day. I didn't need to because it's really easy to remember that brain rest is boring.

December 31st

Tried to leave the house tonight for New Years. I can't drink, and I don't want to drive. I'm exhausted. I'm not sure why I left the house. Leaving the house is overrated.

January 2nd

I went to the car dealership today to start the process of getting a new car. I sat there for an hour, waiting. I should have been home, but I just wanted to feel like I accomplished something. I need to make sub plans for my students tomorrow and maybe even Thursday.

I can't believe how exhausting it is to do the most basic things. I feel fine when I'm at home. Once I'm out, it's like I'm in a fog. I feel like everything I'm doing is for the first time, as if my muscle memory was wiped. I remember doing these things, just can't seem to do any of it right. The muscle relaxants make it easier to move, but I still feel that piercing pain when I turn my head at even half normal speed.

Yesterday, the remote fell off the couch and made a loud crack sound as it landed on the wooden floor. In that moment, I was back in my car. Scared and alone. Heart racing, frozen from fear. In that moment, I realized that I did lose consciousness. The phone ringing brought me back to focus, but I was miles away in the seconds before. How many times did the phone ring before I was aware?

I managed to have a conversation today when two people were talking at the same time without cringing in pain trying to focus. I have no clue what one of them said. I only managed to follow the other. Hopefully, it wasn't anything important.

In so many ways, this would be easier if I had a cast or something visibly broken. People could see the progress, see that I'm not quite there, but more importantly, others would know that I was injured. They would know that I didn't walk away from the accident-free and clear. So, they wouldn't tell me how thankful they are I wasn't hurt. I know they mean well, but I'm too tired to explain. More importantly, I would be able to see and gauge my own progress. As my cuts and bruises heal and fade, I know how long I'll be left with those marks. I have no way of knowing how long before I feel connected to the rest of my brain again. No way of knowing how long before I don't feel like a stranger in my own body.

What will my doctor say tomorrow, when I ask him if he can give me a cast? Will he understand? Will I feel more detached from the world I no longer understand?

January 6th

I am missing the first 3 days of the semester. I have 75 students, most of whom have never met me, and I'm not there. I hate concussions. I hate headrests and airbags and trees and laws of physics. Brain rest is boring, but at least it's an excuse to block out the rest of the world for a little longer.

January 9th

I'm not ready to go back to work. I'm not ready to leave my house, but today seems just as good a day as any. If there's anything that has kept me from losing it during this time, it is my job. Even after missing the first week back, everyone welcomes me with open arms. Teachers who have given up part or all of their planning periods (in some cases multiple times) to sub for me aren't angry as I would have expected. They are happy to see me return. I don't know why I was so worried. I have the best workplace I could ask for.

I decided I would talk to my students about what is going on with me and my brain. It isn't easy, and I hold back tears at times when telling them about what happened and how it will impact what we are going to be working on for at least the first part of the semester. Several students who have also suffered concussions nod in camaraderie. They get it.

That's what got me through the first day. Then I left and went home to sleep for 12 hours.

This continued. Some days were better, some days weren't.

January 18th

Three weeks #postconcussion and still healing. In the last three weeks, I have learned that the side effects/symptoms of post-concussion are basically that of pregnancy, plus a few fun extras (irritability, exhaustion, nausea, neck pain, tension headaches, ringing ears, hypersensitivity to certain sounds, lack of focus, and crappy memory/processing). I used to get migraines…I would take one instead in a heartbeat.

It is a daily struggle to be patient with myself when I'm not able to do what used to come so easily (or without exhausting me by 10 AM). I do a good enough job of acting like I'm ok, and maybe that's a bad thing. Sometimes it's harder to keep it together. They say it just takes time. I kind of hate hearing about "time" right now.

February 3rd

I made it through an entire week without feeling like I was mentally held back. I have made it through post-concussion.

Then it happened...

February 15th

I presented two 3-hour pre-conference sessions at #METC17 and helped host the #tlap (Teach Like a Pirate) Twitter chat on Monday, then powered through Tuesday's sessions like a pro. I met up with fellow Google Innovators and members of my Twitter PLN. It was a great week. Anyone who knows anything about me knows I live for these days. METC is our "little ISTE of the Midwest," and my goal had been to be well enough for it.

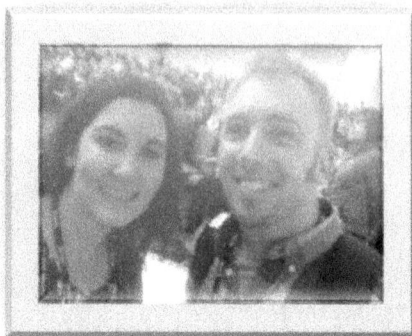

#COL16 mini-reunion with Austin Houp

@METCedplus
METCedplus.org

Getting ready to Teach Like a Pirate with Dave Burgess

I was set to present one last session on Digital Differentiation, and I was ready. I kept joking that I wasn't because I have this thing about tweaking my materials and going perfectionistic on them, but I was ready. I'd been ready for months. Then at 2 PM, my brain decided it was done, but I didn't know it yet.

I walked into my session and began by telling them about my journey, *this journey.* I didn't tell it for sympathy or pity. I told them because it is at the heart of why differentiation and accommodations are good for everyone, not just students who have been identified with learning needs. It's why we should be familiar with them, because students won't always know about the tools that could assist them. I tripped over some of my words, but I was off to a great start.

Then my computer glitched.

I'm the person people come to when there is a tech issue. That is who I have been for years. I know how to troubleshoot most problems, so when I clicked a link in a Google Doc, and nothing happened, I am more than qualified to handle that. Having passed the Google Certified Trainer test means I know how to figure this out. But I couldn't. My ability to problem-solve was gone.

I was instantly overwhelmed by the lights in the room, the temperature, the number of people in the room, the sound of them shifting in their seats. In my classroom, I would have been able to have my students work on something while I sat down and collected my thoughts. Here, in a room with 40+ teachers, I had to be on my game.

My reputation as a speaker, presenter, trainer, teacher, conference committee member...that depends on me being able to collect my thoughts, focus, sound like I know what I'm talking about and generally, finish what I start. When every part of me wanted to say, "here's the link, go have fun," I stepped away from my computer and tried to share some stories from my classroom, some from previous years, and some from now. It was the worst session I've ever led. It's embarrassing. Even days (and months) later, I fixated on it because I know I can do better, I know I am capable of better. But in that moment, I wasn't.

All I want to do is go back in time and make those 50 minutes better, but I can't. All I can hope is those in attendance learned something that made my session worth attending for them.

October 27th

A new school year is in full swing. I watch football and soccer games with a much different perspective now. When one of the players goes down or takes a hit, I find myself holding my breath and saying a silent prayer that they won't have to experience what I have. Some of them know their concussion number well, others can only guess.

Most days, I don't get little reminders about my concussion. I still tend to overwork myself and not get enough sleep. That's when it all comes back. Today was one of those days. It's still amazing to me that my doctors can say it was a mild concussion, and yet I experience post-concussion syndrome symptoms even months later. I have no doubt my job contributes highly to this.

For that reason, this is the year of me focusing on self-care. I have a set of priorities and get done what needs to be done, then I take time to chill. Being a connected educator makes it difficult to turn off the screens. I'm used to feeling productive, but I'm getting used to the idea of taking a break from everything (in fact, sometimes I break for *way* longer than I should).

Today, I lost the ability to focus on anything with a screen or words to read by 10AM, needed to turn the lights off, and powered through the last half of my school day by avoiding anything with a screen or bright light. My students actually enjoy working by natural light (we have amazing windows), so it's nice that I don't have to explain every time we turn off the fluorescents. All I really have to do is ask, "Do we want to work with the lights off today," which is good because it still bothers me when I can't operate at 200% capacity all the time.

On really bad days, my mind goes blank when talking to a student, and I have trouble recalling their names. Those days are the hardest. I don't like acknowledging my limitations, but in some way, I've come to appreciate that I now have a definitive limit when my brain tells me when I need a break. Where I used to power through, I now pause.

So, what's this really about?

So many things. Here are a couple of them:

One

When I met with my new primary care physician in January, he told me that he is seeing kids take about **twice** as long to recover from concussions since schools are going 1:1 and cell phones are more prevalent. The refresh rate is very taxing on the brain. That's why screen time must be limited, ideally eliminated during recovery.

Looking at a screen is your job description when you teach technology, and I fully understand the risk and setback I cause myself by subjecting my brain to endless hours of lesson planning, personal learning, and tinkering with new technology. Our students don't always have a choice. I often have not even known when a student has come back to school following a concussion.

It's my personal goal to do better and lay out some recommendations for students who have suffered brain trauma when returning to the classroom. If just one good thing could come from my experience, it will be that.

Two

I share this because I'm not the only person you know who has an invisible injury. You can't see all wounds, and everyone is different. Some are better at hiding the pain. Some may know what tools are available to help them on a daily basis, others may not. Teachers often provide a support system without ever realizing it.

This was a rough year for a lot of people in many ways. It has been blamed for taking a lot of people from us. I refuse to let it take me too.

About the Author

Stephanie Filardo

Stephanie Filardo is a Google Certified Educator and Innovator, Nearpod Author, and frequent conference presenter who has previously taught math and special education at the elementary, middle, and high school levels. Her current position includes teaching technology/computer science classes at St. John Vianney High School in St. Louis, Missouri. She uses technology to differentiate and take new approaches to the curriculum. Stephanie blogs at i3algebra.blogspot.com and tweets at @i3algebra.

Blogging in Today's Classroom

Stephanie D. Jacobs

A personal story

> **Dedicated to the memory of Mary Little Hudson****

One day, rather unexpectedly, my former staff and I found ourselves dealing with the death of a co-worker, a teacher assistant, and friend to many. In the midst of dealing with so many emotions, my remedy was to go home and write. And so, I did.

After publishing my blog post, receiving feedback, and reading the comments, I learned that many of us shared the same feelings and emotions in that moment. We connected. As a leader, I came away with a very valuable lesson that day, "never forget to just be human." This blog post is no longer published, and I have since created another blog (another lesson: be sure you own the email address connected to your blog). I would like to share it here.

*Our hearts are heavy today, but Heaven is
rejoicing. Heaven gained an Angel. What
next? How do we handle it? What are the
answers? Write. Writing is my therapy.
Nothing could have prepared me for this day.
No amount of schooling, training, or even life
experiences. I was not prepared for that
panicked announcement for me to report to
the front office. I was not prepared for that
phone call. I was not prepared, but required
to act. In times of crisis, it is great to have
support. In the days ahead, that word will
become our comfort. Support. We must
support each other, especially in difficult
times. Just yesterday, our main priority was
focused on curriculum and copies (Copies?
We were talking about copies--#AIreference).
Today, we realized what's truly important in
life. Cherish each other. Cherish those
moments with kids. Give them good memories.
That's what we have to hold on to now. Good
memories. During our session today with grief
counselors, they offered the following advice:
*Crayons and a piece of paper-how you start
the dialogue with kids
*Don't be afraid to show your emotions
Be open and honest

*Listen
*Share comfort food with each other
*Share stories/remember the good times
*Create an award in memory of
Today was an unusually quiet day at school.
The kids could tell, something is amiss. If only
they knew how much those hugs meant today.
The questions will come tomorrow, and we
will provide two things: presence and
availability. That's what they will need.
That's what we need. After a long, rough day
today, when I heard the words, "I put the sign
out!" I held out hope for a minute, maybe a
second, and then reality set in. It wasn't her.
And then, tears. #RIPmary

Even as I share this years later, it is still
emotional. In that moment, it hurt. But we all
found comfort in these words...in this simple
blog post. It allowed us to have dialogue and
know that it was okay to hurt together, to
fellowship together, to cry together, and even (as
memories were shared) laugh together.

Initially, I wanted to use blogging as my way
to capture and reflect on my year(s) as an
administrator. Many of my first blogging posts
were centered around content that I learned from

my training in our state's Principal Induction
program. During that year, I discovered that
blogging was also my form of therapy. Thank you
for allowing me to take you on a brief journey
into one particular experience during my time as
an administrator.

What is blogging?

A blog can be a powerful tool. You decide
the purpose. You decide the topic(s), and you
decide the audience in most cases. This platform
is a way to develop your writing skills. It can be a
tool for reflection. A blog can also be your
connection to the world as you build your
audience and routinely share your thoughts. Keep
an open mind when developing your blog. Just
because you are an educator doesn't mean that
you must write about education-related topics.
That is another great thing about blogging. You
get to pick your own lane. Write about your
interests: gardening, photography, cooking, arts &
crafts, and more!

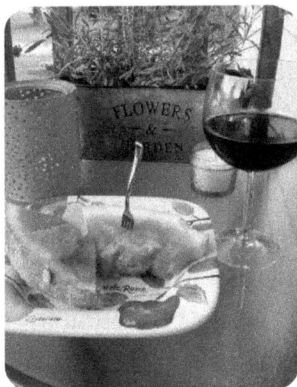

(Photo credit: Vanessa Jacobs)

There are also a variety of platforms to use for writing and sharing your blog. When deciding which to use, pick the one that best fits your style, needs, and level of comfort. In the process, you may want to research and read some other blogs from a few of your favorite Edustars to see what styles you like best. To get you headed in the right direction, I will share a few here.

Blogger: Includes free hosting of your blog content. Connects directly to your Google account. Allows users to upload or embed media.

Edublogs: A platform for creating student blogs for your entire class. There are free and paid versions for more storage space and other features.

Weebly: May be used to turn your blog into a website or online store. Contains drag and drop features when creating posts. There are free and paid versions.

WordPress: Provides options for blogs and websites as well as free and paid versions. Allows users to upload or embed media.

Wix: This is another option for turning your blog into a website. Features include blog editor, photo gallery, and a variety of additional tools.

Edustars: Who's Who? I would recommend the following blogs/bloggers to get you started:

**Stephanie Jacobs:
www.thisblogiswhy.blogspot.com (My blog, of course!)
Cara Carroll:
www.thefirstgradeparade.org
Amanda Rider:
www.cupcakesandlessonplans2.blogspot.com
Latoya Dixon:
www.leadershipwithlatoya.org**

The Compelled Tribe

Jennifer Hogan:
www.thecompellededucator.com
Craig Vroom: **www.fueling-education.com**

Jon Wennstrom:
www.sparkoflearning.blogspot.com

These blogs are just a few of my favorites, and they can give you an idea of how to shape your blog, depending on your audience and/or purpose. Some teachers share content and resources through Teachers Pay Teachers via their blog. Your blog may also spotlight your podcast or a Twitter chat group. Blogs can focus on home projects or your role as a leader. Take some time and look through the Compelled Tribe bloggers for a more extensive listing of Edustars. You will be able to access links by visiting the pages of Hogan, Vroom, and Wennstrom.

Student Blogging

Usually, when I present at conferences on this topic, my audience is a mix of educators who want to become bloggers themselves, and those who want their students to become bloggers. I strongly believe in building blogging tribes, which essentially means that everyone is blogging: students and teachers. What better way to support each other in the learning/writing process? Now, while you may not become a daily blogger, there is still value in gaining knowledge that you can share with your students to have meaningful dialogue. Many of the same platforms that I mentioned previously can also be used with students depending on your level.

Quick note: be sure to read privacy policies or terms and conditions before you begin your work. Some additional tools that may be more user-friendly for younger writers:

Kidblog: Teacher-friendly option that connects with Google products. Includes lesson plans and resources. Teachers monitor and control student activity.

Seesaw: Presented as a student work portfolio that includes a blog component. For younger users, they may record, draw, or upload content to their blog posts.

You will find that there is a multitude of lessons to be taught while introducing blogs into the curriculum, for example, writing/editing content, voice, and responding to your peers. Instructors will want to focus on awareness of your online identity, digital citizenship, and citing sources. Blogging in today's classroom encourages breaking down those four walls and expanding the educational experiences for your students and educators as well. You can connect with other classrooms across the country or globally. Educators can easily collaborate with authors, speakers, and other professionals with just a few clicks. Share your vision and goals with others and watch your connections begin to grow.

Develop your students as true global leaders by building and shaping their voices through blogging. If you are looking for a way to broaden your reach, start with the hashtag #comment4kids on Twitter. Your students can receive feedback/comments from an authentic audience. Start a conversation!

Which subject matters best lend themselves to blogging? All! Think about having students create a blog journal from the Revolutionary War period, create a vlog (video blog) explaining how to work a difficult math problem, or create a food journal that demonstrates healthy eating choices for a week. The possibilities are endless.

Blogging with Professional Growth in Mind

Whether you decide to become a blogger or just shape your students into young writers, keep an open mind. Think growth and possibilities. Defy limitations.

I know I feel as though blogging has opened a new world for me as an educator. There is so much to learn, so many Edustars to connect with, and a wealth of great resources that can be accessed with the click of your mouse. You can be a part of that culture of lifelong learning that we often hear when discussing our students.

The term that I have connected with as a blogger is *branding*. Some may view this term in a negative light, but I think it is important. Anything that I attach my name to, anywhere, is a part of my personal/professional brand. It tells people who I am. It tells my story. It is important as a blogger (teacher or student) that you tell your story, that you own your story. What is the image that you want others to view when your name flashes across their screen or slides across that desk?

How can blogging become your professional growth tool?

- Become a reader. Read other blogs (professional, hobbies, student-friendly, etc.).
- Share about conferences that you attend.
- Present at conferences on a topic you are passionate about.
- Share the great things happening in your classroom/school.
- Share resources or tools that you love.
- Share your personal/professional story.

I started telling you a little about my story at the beginning of this chapter. That chapter of my life closed with "Class," and that became a part of my brand. In the late days of my time as an administrator, I heard daily from those around me that I continued to carry myself with even in adversity. That was the lesson that I strived to share with my team. No matter the situation, handle yourself with dignity, grace, and class. In those moments MsClassNSession was born. Then, she transformed as I became more empowered through my blog. Not only was it a personal journal, but it has become my avenue for sharing with the world.

About the Author

Stephanie D. Jacobs

Stephanie D. Jacobs is a 19-year veteran in education who resides in Rock Hill, SC. Stephanie is currently an Instructional Technology Coach. Her background includes teaching in grades PreK-5, as well as serving two years as an elementary school principal and Internship Supervisor at Winthrop University, respectively. Stephanie also serves as an adjunct instructor at York Technical College in Reading. She is passionate about education and shares her passion through blogging and presenting at a variety of educational conferences. Let's connect!

Twitter: **https://twitter.com/msclassnsession**
Blog: **http://thisblogiswhy.blogspot.com**
Website: **www.msclassnsession.weebly.com**

On the Top: My Life as a Swim Practice

Kelly Grotrian

How a background in coaching swimming made me the teacher I am today

Once upon a time, I was a swim coach and long before that (OK, not that long), I was a competitive swimmer. These two roles greatly shaped the teacher I have become, and I'm happy to say I wouldn't have it any other way. Coaches I had growing up, swim friends, and non-friends alike; these are what made me the teacher I am today. Just as a swim practice is constant back and forth in the pool, so, too, is the life of a teacher - constant back and forth in a very cyclical motion.

For those unfamiliar with the world of competitive swimming, the phrase "on the top" refers to the analog clock or stopwatch. The top of the clock is also known as the 60, so you might hear "we're leaving on the 60!" This refers to when the first swimmer is to leave the wall to begin their set or distance assigned by the coach. Here is where my story begins, on the top.

A Brief Overview of a Swim Practice (from the Perspective of a Swimmer)

1. Awkwardly get completely undressed in the locker room and wiggle into your swimsuit. I say wiggle because those suckers can literally suck the life out of you! Talk about tight!
2. Make sure you have your cap and goggles, perhaps more than one of each in case they break during practice - this has been known to happen.
3. If you care at all about your feet - wear sandals from the locker room to the pool deck.
4. Arrive on the pool deck and make your way to your lane. Swimmers are grouped in lanes based on their speed. I was a fan of going last in my lane to minimize someone tapping my feet.

5. Fix your hair, cap, and goggles for as long as possible. You know that water is freezing, and you want to delay entry as long as possible. Insert teammate who decides to push you in anyway - ugh!
6. Attentively listen to your coach while simultaneously hanging on the lane line or continuing to fix/play with your cap and goggles.
7. So much for this being a brief overview.
8. Partake in the warm-up phase of practice. As indicated by the name, you are warming up your body because a) the water is freezing and b) seriously the water is so cold.
9. The next one-and-a-half to two hours can get a little tricky. Here is where the coach gives you your sets/main sets, and you may or may not feel like your body is going to collapse. Swimming is the only sport I know that utilizes every single muscle at the same time. To not engage your full body at all times could result in you laying at the bottom of the pool!

Now that you know the basics, here are some more details about practice that aren't as easy to see.

You see, while I was born a fish, I wasn't the fastest fish. I didn't enjoy the pain I felt both in my lungs and my body - I liked being in the water, once warmed up. However, the vast majority of my swimming career I loathed practice.

If you've never seen a swim practice, it's quite riveting. Back and forth, back and forth, and yet again, back and forth… for a few hours. To an onlooker, this seems monotonous and boring - not to mention when the swimmers start only using one arm or using breaststroke arms with butterfly legs! You might wonder if the swimmers had an actual stroke based on what some of our drills look like! But never fear, there is always a method to the madness in swimming.

Some days practices were manageable and fun, other days it was grueling and incredibly painful. I write this from the perspective of a swimmer and swim coach.

I'm not entirely sure how I fell into coaching, as it happened at the ripe age of 16 for my summer team, but I took to coaching like yet another fish takes to water. I loved it. As I mentioned earlier, I wasn't the fastest, but you could photograph or record my races to use as models for technique. I cared about doing everything right, clearly.

Being on the pool deck versus being in the pool presents a new set of challenges. I've coached at outdoor pools as well as indoor pools with close to 20 kids in each lane. If you think managing a classroom of twenty kids is hard, try adding the element of water and about 60 other noisy splashers!

A Brief Overview of a Swim Practice (from the Perspective of a Coach)

1. Wear something you don't mind getting soaking wet from all the splashing.
   a. This includes sensible shoes/sandals, as the deck will be wet and you don't want to fall down! I've slid on many occasions while coaching indoors.
2. Determine what you want to work on with your swimmers today.

a. Consider what you worked on previously, what still needs improvement, and whether you have a meet coming up as this may dictate the practice a bit more.

    i. Think of a meet like you would a summative assessment.

3. Depending on the age level you're working with, you may want to write out the day's workout so that each lane has a copy.

a. Older swimmers will be able to follow along on a more complicated set.

b. If you go this route, I recommend typing up your "plan" and printing a copy for each lane.

4. Arrive at the pool with enough time to set up.

a. Depending on your situation, this may include lane lines (which the swimmers can help with), grabbing kickboards, pull buoys, etc.

5. Greet your swimmers as they emerge from the locker room and give them a few minutes to put their caps and goggles on - but be clear that you're starting the warm-up portion of the workout in X-number of minutes, so they better be ready!
6. Swimmers should be able to complete your warm-up unassisted as this is not a time for instruction (just the instruction to get in the water and go!).
7. Once the warm-up has been completed and your shoes are thoroughly soaked from the splashing, you're ready to begin your first set!

While swimming may have prepared me to coach, coaching definitely prepared me to teach. The bare bones of coaching and teaching are the same - you have to plan, you have to execute, and you have to care. But coaching swimming, specifically, made me the type of teacher that I am today.

Imagine your child is attending their first swim practice and you're all set on the bleachers to watch attentively and provide emotional support. Your child has their suit, cap, and goggles ready to go and they can't wait to get in the water and please both you and their coaches! It's an exhilarating feeling to watch your child go off and swim! Suddenly, you see the coach enter the water - not the swimmers. And for the next two hours, the coach is swimming, talking, swimming, talking, and not once do the actual swimmers enter the water. They are to quietly sit on the side of the pool and watch their coach. Bummer.

But think about it, some teachers do this exact same thing - they get in and swim instead of letting the swimmers practice. There was a time when nearly every teacher was a "lecture-teacher." I can remember my 8th-grade history teacher who used to fill his chalkboards with notes and then sat and talked at us for the entire period. I never did get any direction on whether I was supposed to copy down those notes. I definitely remember writing notes to my friends during class though (this was pre-texting days when we actually had to use pen/paper and discretely pass the note across the room). It's amazing I ended up teaching history myself with the examples I had!

Lecture-based teachers are doing all the work. The students become passive participants in the "show" (I don't even think I should use the word participants since they're really just sitting there). I get it, I understand why some teachers prefer to lecture. I've heard some teachers say it's "easier" to just lecture, that they are the teacher so therefore they should impart the knowledge. But again, I ask you to think about the coach swimming during practice instead of the swimmers. No one joins a team to watch the coach participate in the sport - you join a team so that YOU can participate. Classroom settings should be the same. Let the students participate, let the swimmers swim.

I can feel myself going into my "Back to School Night" speech as I write this, but I truly and firmly believe that lecture-based instruction is a dated practice and should be abandoned when possible. How do I teach then if not to directly instruct my students?

I do exactly what I started doing when I was 16 as a swim coach to a herd of 9- and 10-year-olds.

Effective coaching, like effective teaching, is about presenting a skill, modeling accordingly, and then "letting the fish swim." I mention modeling because there's a difference between that and "lecturing" or swimming the entire practice yourself while others watch. I used the tools I was given (some of those tools being actual swimmers) and broke the skills down piece by piece and allowed a swimmer/student to model the correct action. I needed to be describing the action as it happened, not the one doing the action. This also stands to attest that I don't need to be the "sage on the stage" and that others are capable too - like my swimmers and my students. How great they must've felt when I asked a few of them to demonstrate a flip-turn instead of doing it myself!

To continue this analogy further, when I taught my swimmers how to do a flip-turn, I compared it to something I knew many of them were already familiar with - somersaults! How did we start learning how to flip? By doing somersaults in the water! How many can you do without taking a breath? Can you do it without using your arms out at your side? I made it FUN. The practiced part of the skill in a FUN way.

From there, we discussed how flip-turns are basically half-somersaults and that you have to land your feet on the wall because that's how you'll push off and continue swimming your race. So, what did we do next? We practiced a somersault, near the wall, and made sure our feet hit the wall - once they hit the wall, they stop!

As this chapter is not a learn-to-swim course, I will leave the analogy there. But I had to mix direct instruction, if you will, with swimmer/student activities. I used the tools that I had, I made connections so that my swimmers/students would understand the concept, and I gave them time to work. This is exactly how my classes have run since I started teaching twelve years ago.

A Brief Overview of a Lesson (from the Perspective of a Teacher)

1. Wake-up and complete your morning routine/ritual which may or may not include planning out today's lesson in the shower.
2. Be sure to have breakfast, because you're going to need your energy!
3. Wiggle into your outfit and be sure to look professional (am I the only teacher who would prefer to operate in sweats and sneakers?!).
4. Drive to school, which may or may not include continuing to plan out today's lesson.
   a. Watch out for deer on the road though - stay focused on the road at all times!

5. Arrive at school (if you're like me, you're one of the first five people in the building) and figure out if you need copies and book like all hell to the copy room in hopes that a line has not already begun to form.

   a. Again, if you're like me, you're still running to the copy room... and then have to unlock it and wait for the machines to warm-up. Ahh! Another warm-up!

6. If you do not need copies, then your Google Slides need to be made - because again, you were planning on the way into school. But it's OK because you're super early, so you have the time to add in your Bitmojis, et cetera.

7. Greet your students at the door with a smile and hope that they at least look back at you or respond (as a secondary teacher, sometimes I'm lucky if they even look back - especially first thing in the morning).

8. Encourage students to start the "Do Now," if they haven't already, and get ready to teach your lesson!

Again, I told you my lessons - my teaching style - greatly mirrors what I went through as a swimmer and a coach. I'm not going to stand up in front of my class and lecture for 42 minutes because it's easier if I just tell the kids about Rosa Parks. If I did that, the pool-equivalent of listening to that lecture would be kids drifting off to the deep end, spitting water at each other, or asking to leave to go to the bathroom. The only way students will feel engaged in a lesson is if they're actually engaged - doing something! They only way a swimmer will learn how to do a flip-turn is if they're actually flipping in the water and hopefully not smacking their heads on the wall as they try (it happens - hopefully, there's enough hair in their cap to cushion the blow!).

So, am I ever "on the top?" Sometimes. As a swimmer, I would have races where I earned my best time - so then I was on the top of my game. As a coach, I would have meets wherein we won, even a few undefeated seasons under my belt - so then I was on top of my game. As a teacher, I have had successful lessons or had students come back and tell me how much they appreciated my willingness to work with them - so then I felt on top of my game.

But just as that hand on the clock goes round and round, just as a swimmer goes back and forth, and just as every September I start over with the dropping of the Atomic Bomb - sometimes I'm on the top, and sometimes I'm not…but there's always another shot to make it right at the next 60!

About the Author

Kelly Grotrian

Kelly Grotrian has been teaching American History in the East Brunswick Public School District (in East Brunswick, NJ) since January 2007. While she does not define herself as a "history nerd," she prefers the term "activity designer" or "activity enthusiast." Throughout her career, Kelly has taught 8th Grade Early American History, Psychology I, US History II, and AP American History. She loves the events leading to the Civil War unit and has a plethora of analogies that go along with that unit - namely how "the seeds of the Civil War were planted at the signing of the Declaration of Independence" and how "compromises are like band-aids."

Kelly's love for teaching again does not come from a love of content, but a love of learning and creating methods by which anyone can take an interest in historic topics and events. Kelly did not find a "love" of history until college! But the love of teaching began as a swim coach back in 1998 for the Maplewood Makos Summer Swim Team. She lasted as coach from that time until 2014 when she had to hang up her whistle, stopwatch, and clipboard due to her commitment to providing the best learning experience for her students.

In addition to teaching and coaching, Kelly is presently working her way to becoming an administrator, obtaining her certificates to become a principal and supervisor by June 2018. While she enjoys teaching and working with students, she has aspirations to work as an administrator and impact students and teachers from an administrative level.

Kelly is most known in her district for creating the Video-Based Question activity, which has circulated greatly beyond East Brunswick at this point. She found that student engagement increased when newer technology was brought into the classroom and found that the use of video allowed students to control the pace of their own learning. Kelly is always seeking new ways to bring history to life for her students and believes that everyone can learn if given the proper tools.

i carry your heart

Marialice B.F.X. Curran, PhD

When they know we care, they'll move mountains.

I've carried this e.e. cummings[13] poem in my heart for years. Wherever I go, it's gone with me, much like the students I have known over the years.

One particular student, I'll call him Frank (that's my dad's name), has had the most significant influence on my personal and professional life. I was teaching middle school back in 1998, and my dad was having an operation just before our December break. A substitute covered for me, and my students knew why I was starting my break early...not too many details, but enough that they knew I'd be at the hospital with my family before Christmas. They made cards, bought a maroon blanket for my dad (maroon for Boston College – we're a big BC family), and had parents drop off meals-on-

---

13

https://www.poetryfoundation.org/poetrymagazine/browse?
contentId=49493

wheels for us in the waiting room. The gesture, to this day, still fills me with raw emotion.

Things did not go as planned and my dad ended up in the hospital for 59 days. That's a lot of days to be out, but I tried my best to go back to school as often as possible. One day, Frank was wound up during homeroom and just *had* to go to the office. I was barely hanging on and really have no idea why he had to go to the office. Without any questions, I just let him go.

I was teaching Frank's class during the lunch block…the very worst block to every teach – the first twenty-ish minutes the students can't think about anything but lunch, and the second twenty-ish minutes after lunch they are focused on what happened during lunch. It's always been my least favorite block of time to teach. On that day, Frank could not settle the first half of the block. Then the front office called and asked for Frank to come down.

When Frank came back to class, he was carrying a bouquet of flowers with a message that read, "Don't worry Miss Curran, your father will be alright because he has a daughter like you."

Putting the pieces together, I learned that once Frank saw me that morning, he was determined to have flowers delivered to school to cheer me up. He had the front office call for the delivery and had left his hard-earned paper route money to pay for it.

It is this exact moment that has been etched into my heart which I continue to carry with me because when I came back to school after February vacation, I was a changed person. I had lost my dad and had to face my students. My most powerful lesson happened that day. I didn't worry about trying to catch them up. Instead, I opened my heart to them and taught them the most valuable life lesson I could. I said something like this, "Today you need to tell someone I love you, thank you, I'm sorry, because all we have as a guarantee is today."

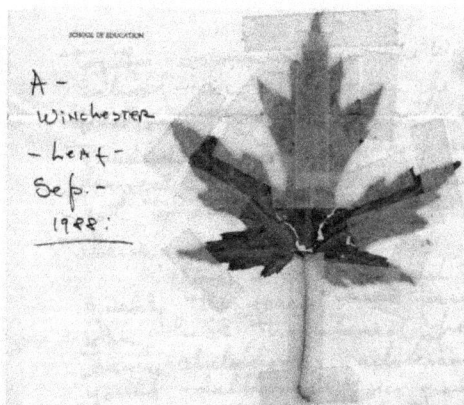

I took out a letter written by my dad on September 24, 1988 and began to read. I've carried this letter with me for years and have shared it with many students. It has a leaf taped to the worn letterhead. I'm sure it was a bright and colorful leaf when I first opened it in '88, but it is now brown and fragile. The letter reads:

My dearest Marialice:
Yesterday, I opened the door of the family room and lying there before me was this beautiful leaf. Somehow it reminded me of you! The many fall days we would leave together on our way to the Washington School or McCall or the high school. How many times have both of us trundled through so many beautiful leaves but in our anxiousness to get to school have never noticed them? Mom and I both said today how quickly the years have passed as you have transitioned from infancy – early childhood and adolescence into young adulthood. Your growth has happened so quickly that perhaps I have not been attentive enough to tell you how proud I am of you. As some tree has to be proud of this leaf, this father is proud of his DAUGHTER. You have become everything that I could ever hope for!

The letter continues talking about Town Day and the parade and his hope that the Red Sox would win the World Series that year. I cry every time I read it, and I certainly cried the day I read it to my students.

I asked them to use the class time to write a letter to someone. They took the assignment very seriously and were deeply engaged from the moment they started writing. In sharing my dad's letter, I explained how having a handwritten letter is like owning a piece of that person, like a piece of history, carrying them in your heart forever.

What Frank did for me that day is a reminder to all of us about the importance of building relationships and culture in our classroom. Our students don't really care what we know, they care how much we care and when they know we care, they'll move mountains.

So, for all my students back in 1998, especially Frank, "i carry your heart with me (i carry it in my heart)."

About the Author

Marialice B.F.X. Curran, PhD

Dr. Marialice B.F.X. Curran is the Founder and CEO of the Digital Citizenship Institute. Her advanced graduate and doctoral studies on adolescent development at Boston College reinforced her commitment to service learning as Dr. Curran leads by hand, heart, and mind. As a mother and a connected educator, she has served as an associate professor, middle school teacher, principal, and library media specialist.

As a pioneer in digital citizenship, she developed and created the first 3-credit digital citizenship course for teachers in the United States. She co-founded the digital citizenship chat on Twitter (2011) and the Digital Citizenship Summit (2015). She serves on the leadership team for the International Society for Technology in

Education (ISTE) Digital Citizenship PLN and is a researcher, keynote, international speaker and TEDxYouth speaker.

An entrepreneur and puppeteer at the age of 11, Dr. Curran's experiences include world travel with a particular interest in the creative arts, middle-level education, special education, teacher education and educational technology. Dr. Curran is committed to promoting social good using social media and technology. She believes in a community-driven approach to educating and empowering digital citizens to create solutions in local, global and digital communities. Her mission is to turn negatives into positives and help to transform participants into designers, creative thinkers, global collaborators, problem solvers, and justice-oriented digital citizens.

She has partnered with her eleven-year-old son, and the two are a recognized professionally as a mother/son digital citizenship team. The dynamic duo model best practices while working with parents, educators, students, and community organizations.

Follow Marialice on Twitter at @mbfxc and @digcitinstitute, @digcitsummit, and @digcitkids.

What are the Qualities and Characteristics of a Dynamic Leader?

Josue Falaise, Ed.D.

The qualities and characteristics of a dynamic leader

Dynamic schools are dynamic because the leader and the entire school community have collectively invested time and energy beyond the call of duty to make it dynamic. The leader must have effective listening skills and offer many platforms for staff to provide input. More importantly, the leader must believe in his/her colleagues and implement decisions from collaborative feedback. The leader must constantly put the needs of the constituents and staff before his/her own. Moreover, s/he sacrifices countless hours of personal time for the benefit of the school community.

The leader highlights the strengths of individuals, so they can further contribute to the innovation of the school. The leader identifies areas of challenge to design professional development plans geared to strengthen the staff collectively. He/she encourages and finds creative ways for staff with areas of challenge to connect to staff with strengths in those areas to grow as a professional learning community (PLC).

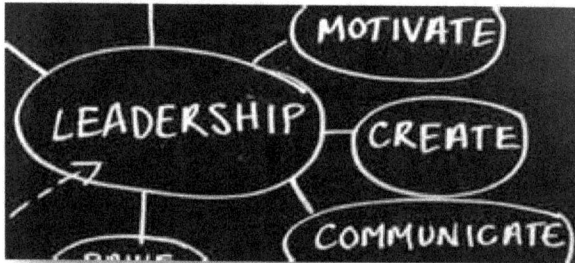

Despite the school community working collaboratively, the leader is faced with unique situations daily. S/he must be a thought-provoker and problem-solver that thinks outside the box to address daily problems, especially when there are no easy answers. S/he must work with the staff to find a solution to each problem, even when some people believe it is very difficult, to nearly impossible.

Behind each dynamic school community, a leader is leading by example. S/he is aware that everyone is watching his/her behavior with scrutiny and response to situations. Therefore, responses to urgent matters and chaos are dealt prudently and calmly. S/he carries him/herself professionally and with dignity inside and outside the school community. The leader does not accept mediocrity. S/he provides clear expectations for every position, including students. Policies and procedures are established to address each situation and hold everyone accountable to the highest standard. His/her work ethic is inimitable.

As a novice administrator, I consistently dreamed of becoming a dynamic leader and transforming the professional landscape of underperforming schools to becoming high performing. When I initially became principal of my current school six years ago, the school had a stigma for student, staff, and teaching challenges. In a matter of one year, we made significant strides towards becoming a high performing/dynamic school. One of the first things we did was visit a few schools that were considered in that category. Then our school leadership council (SLC) comprising teachers, parents, support staff, community member, and administration developed a collaborative vision, core belief statements, and goals. We selected four key topics and designed an action plan to address them. Then the culture of the school immediately began to change.

Although I had high expectations for staff, they began to add more expectations for themselves and their peers. Teachers with specific skills were highlighted, and they began leading job-embedded professional opportunities like faculty meetings and the PLCs.

All staff members were able to participate in decisions about the school's function through various committees like SLC, data, safety, PBIS, discipline, multicultural, wellness, open house, et cetera. Teachers elected a PLC leader who facilitated meetings of curriculum revisions, analysis of student academic performance data to drive instruction, instructional and assessment interventions, literature review, discussing researched-based best practices, and innovative practices observed during peer classroom walkthroughs, et cetera.

To answer my topical question, I believe the role of a leader in a dynamic school community requires effective listening skills, selflessness, understanding individual strengths and areas of challenges, problem-solving skills, holding others accountable, leading by example and making those around him/her better. After 14 years of being a school building leader, I am even more confident that these quintessential leadership qualities and characteristics are needed to lead a dynamic school or school system. Do these characteristics or qualities describe you partially or entirely?

Aspiring and current administrators seeking to be dynamic leaders should take heed to the following three perceptual challenges associated with dynamic leaders and schools.

1) Transformation will not occur overnight:

Since a school community does not become dynamic overnight, the leader must be patient with the timing of the transformation. Each school community is different. Everyone must always remember the goal is to continually improve and sustain the student and school performance, adult collaboration, and educators' practice.

2) Fame and money are not guaranteed:

There are examples of leaders who have been able to receive the greatest accolades and even cash in on their school's success. However, this is not the norm. Remember we got into this profession to change the lives of children to better their future. As administrators, we are building the professional capacity of teachers and support staff to improve teaching, adult learning and student learning. Don't be disappointed if you don't win an award for your work/passion. When you have one or more former students coming to you years later displaying how their life was changed because of your diligence and perseverance, there is evidence of your everlasting impact. He or she will most likely pay it forward in the same or different manner.

3) Dynamic schools are not problem-free:

When you hear about a school's success, chances are they are already in the groove of success and worked out most challenges like staff buy-in before the publicity because everyone wants to be part of a success story. So, two important questions to ask those leaders are, "What are some of the past challenges you faced initially as the leader of this school community?" and, "what are your current challenges?"

Ultimately, the climate of dynamic schools portrays the hard work of both the leader and school community. So, it should be noted that support staff members, teachers, students, and parents are also the dynamic leaders actively involved in the successful practices and events occurring at each dynamic school.

About the Author

Josue Falaise, Ed.D.

Dr. Josue Falaise is the founder and CEO of Gomo Educational Services, LLC. He began his 19-year career as an elementary school science teacher. Then he became a middle and high school biology and environmental science teacher. After a short number of years of teaching and time as an adjunct professor at Mercer County Community College, he spent the last 15 years as an administrator in the roles of vice principal, principal and Chief Academic Officer. Most of his career has been in urban school districts.

In addition to his full-time job, Dr. Falaise has also been an educational consultant with NJPSA/FEA for several years presenting on various educational topics like designing curriculum, analyzing data to drive instruction, and developing high performing PLCs throughout the state of New Jersey to schools, districts, and colleges. Follow him on Twitter at @josuefalaise and @GomoEdS.

Transforming Education One Mindset at a Time

Dan Kreiness

If you can allow change to occur, and if you make growth happen, then you may know what it's like to have your "why make you cry."

Unless you are a new educator, you might think the only thing that remains constant in education, is that nothing remains constant in education. Change occurs so often it is sometimes hard for educators to keep up. Educational policies and practices change, assessments change, personnel changes, technology changes. Heck, the students in our classrooms change every year, and even the changes *they* undergo throughout a school year can be rather astonishing.

Coping with all of these changes can sometimes feel overwhelming, until someone takes it upon himself or herself to lead a change effort. Actually, "effort" is a great word to use. Change does take effort. It requires someone to

realize the need for it and to take action to alter it.
That action is synonymous with leadership. As a
matter of fact, a 2017 Business News Daily article
listed "the pursuit of bettering your environment"
number one on a list of eleven ways to define
leadership (Post, 2017).[14] In other words,
someone becomes a leader when they enter into
that pursuit. My goal for this chapter is to explain
how people can use transformational leadership to
undertake and drive such change efforts, whether
they are in education or not.

What is Transformational Leadership?

Transformational leadership is a style of
leadership where a leader works with his or her
followers to identify needed change, creating a
vision to guide the change through inspiration,
and executing the change in tandem with
committed members of the group. The concept of
transformational leadership was first introduced
by James V. Downton, the first to coin the term

---

[14] (2017, September 21). How to Define Leadership -
Business News Daily. Retrieved December 2, 2017, from
https://www.businessnewsdaily.com/3647-leadership-
definition.html

"transformational leadership" and was later developed further by leadership expert James McGregor Burns in his 1978 book, *Leadership*. Burns defined transformational leadership as a process where "leaders and their followers raise one another to higher levels of morality and motivation." Bernard M. Bass later expanded upon Burns' original ideas to develop what is today referred to as Bass' Transformational Leadership Theory. According to Bass, transformational leadership can be defined based on the impact that a leader has on their followers.

According to Bernard M Bass's 1985 book, *Leadership and Performance Beyond Expectations*, cited in a mindtools.com article called, "Transformational Leadership: Becoming an Inspirational Leader," a transformational leader:

- Is a model of integrity and fairness.
- Sets clear goals.
- Has high expectations.
- Encourages others.
- Provides support and recognition.
- Stirs the emotions of people.
- Gets people to look beyond their self-interest.

- Inspires people to reach for the improbable.[15]

Transformational leadership appeals to me most because it can happen at any level of education - or any field - and can involve many "stakeholders" in a change effort or other process. At a school level, transformational leadership may be initiated by district-level or building-level administrators. It will likely spawn from someone who is forward-thinking and recognizes that unless something new is done soon, there will continue to be more failures than successes. The transformational leader's mission then becomes charting a new course for the school or organization and set a plan in motion like moving pieces in a chess match.

The next step becomes tapping into the vital human resources necessary to fulfill the vision. Transformational leaders utilize their followers' strengths. They begin with a meaningful relationship-building process. Often, this happens long before any new ideas or practices are implemented. However, especially in the case of

---

[15] (n.d.). Transformational Leadership - Leadership Training from MindTools.com. Retrieved December 2, 2017, from https://www.mindtools.com/pages/article/transformational-leadership.htm

leaders or followers who are new to their positions, or if there is an abundance of reluctance or resistance, this may have to be done more strategically and on an ongoing basis.

Again, the goal is to build a team-like environment where staff members feel empowered to involve themselves in collaboratively striving to achieve a collective vision and mission of the school or organization. Therefore, getting to know staff members on individual and personal levels will allow leaders to hone in on their unique and specific passions, interests, talents, and abilities to maximize their potential. Done correctly, transformational leadership at an organizational level can ensure that the chain has strong links that cannot be broken since, although each link is strong on its own, together, they are all supporting the work of the entire chain.

Another aspect of transformational leadership is its transferability to the classroom. Teachers can be and should be transformational leaders in their instructional practices, their classroom management, their preparedness, and in the way they lead their students. Just like school and district leaders harness the unique passions, interests, talents, and abilities of their staff, so can teachers with their students. Hence, teachers should be setting visions for their classes and their students in order to then utilize those individual student strengths.

Teachers can empower their students in many ways. When it comes to classroom management, I have known many teachers to dole out jobs or other responsibilities to students or to even have assistant teachers from time to time. As it relates to preparedness, teachers can do themselves and their students a huge favor when they elicit the students' help in determining what should be learned, and how, in order to reach targeted learning standard (*student voice* and *choice*!).

Regarding leading students, teachers are practicing transformational leadership when they can provide opportunities for the students themselves to lead based on their strengths or interests; when they take an otherwise seemingly disengaged student and inspire them to take the lead in an activity that better connects them with an area of interest.

Finally, teachers are transformational in their classroom when they simply recognize the need for change and act on it, recruiting the help and commitment of their students and perhaps even their colleagues. Transformation (change) is rarely easy. It requires the vision piece that I have already mentioned, but it also necessitates a major mind shift. As the leader, whether in the classroom or not, someone is transformational when they can recognize that this mind shift is the most basic building block on which to build that transformation.

My First Time Being a Transformer

I had probably been living on the University of Connecticut campus less than two weeks before I was approached by some upperclassmen who asked me to consider joining their fraternity. After much hesitation, I reluctantly agreed to join. Somehow, I could tell that the brothers in the fraternity quickly saw something special in me. What I could not know at the time was how many amazing leadership opportunities would present themselves by being a brother in this organization, or how much I would learn about myself and how to lead others. It was not long before I became the pledge class president and, once I became a full-fledged brother in the chapter, began taking on leadership roles.

In my first experience serving in an executive board position, I realized that current communication methods were poor. I updated our chapter's website to include more information and more photos and videos from our events, I created an email listserv whereby all members could communicate with each other more easily, and I made sure that everyone knew how to connect with each other no matter what. What I realized I was doing was strengthening the chapter from within to help us market ourselves to the greater university community.

We were an organization of approximately thirty brothers who always yearned to be one of the most popular and powerful chapters on campus. Sure, we had lots of fun and did lots of good for our university and for our international organization, but we knew we were destined for more. We tried throwing the best parties, competing hard in Greek life events that pitted us against other fraternities, joining as many Greek leadership committees as we could, and, of course, getting the highest grades among the fraternities on campus. We even had some brothers agree to live in the biggest dump of a house you could imagine just so we could have our Greek letters seen and our parties attended, while being located right between two of the hottest bars on campus.

Unfortunately, we found that none of these were helping us grow our membership the way we had hoped. It was not until we started shifting our mindsets that we saw some more positive results. What we realized was that need to change actually started with addressing the organization's internal structure, and then some amazing growth started taking shape.

When I took over as the president (or "Master" as it is known within the organization) of the chapter, I recognized the need for even more internal changes. I made some executive decisions to strengthen the organization, beginning with one that would allow for more input and participation from brothers who did not hold executive board positions. Essentially, I was looking to empower more members of the chapter. My good friend (and roommate) was coincidentally elected to be my vice president (or Lieutenant Master). I tasked him with organizing and leading the minor board; the "chair" positions that were not part of the executive board. He held weekly meetings with the minor board to flesh out ideas and plan for events and would report back to me afterward. It did not take long for some of the most amazing ideas to be brought to the table.

During my year-long term, our brothers created, planned, and held events, including the chapter's inaugural formal dance and successful "Battle of the Bands" philanthropy event, that were not only fun but beneficial to our brothers, our international organization, our university, and the global community. We were starting to realize our potential as a chapter. Another timely coincidence was that our university was looking to build a Greek village to house about a dozen of the most deserving Greek organizations.

Although we were small, after some hard work by some of our brothers, leaders within our international organization, and me, our "little engine that could" chapter secured a house in the new village.

Over the next several years after I graduated, our chapter grew to be one of the biggest and most successful on campus. They had emerged as a leading fraternity in the areas of both academic success and competitions among the Greek organizations. They grew so fast they needed to find additional houses to live in since the one in the Greek village only accommodated fifteen brothers.

When I look back to the leadership opportunities I was afforded and the successes of our chapter during my time in it, I also think about connections I can make to educational leadership. I can see that my current work as an educational leader started while I was a fraternity president in college. I was honing my leadership skills while practicing methods characterized by transformational leadership theory. What I thought was me simply trying to lead the fraternity through a necessary transition was so much more. I was realizing and utilizing the passions and interests, talents and abilities of my brothers. I was inspiring them to buy into OUR vision for the chapter. I was encouraging them to play their own part in helping us fulfill that vision. Just as with teachers and students in education, growth did not happen until enough people possessed the right mindset to think that with a clear vision, some hard work and collaboration, and plenty of support, great things could happen.

Transformational Leadership for Educational Change

Between stints as a coach in my previous district and my current one, I wanted to learn more about how to support teachers and decided to take a massive open online course (MOOC) called "Coaching Teachers: Promoting Changes that Stick." This course provided the first opportunities for me to get introduced to the term "growth mindset." The MOOC, created and facilitated by the Match Education organization, provided participants with many meaningful messages and useful strategies and, most importantly, we learned to use the "growth mindset" concept to support the teachers we work with.

Growth mindset is a term coined by Stanford

University psychologist, Carol Dweck, and made
famous in her 2006 book called *Mindset*.

Dweck's research led her to conclude that
there are two general mindsets people hold when
it comes to dealing with change and growth:
either a fixed mindset or a growth mindset.
According to Dweck's accompanying website, in
a fixed mindset, people believe their basic
qualities, like their intelligence or talent, are
simply fixed traits. They spend their time
documenting their intelligence or talent instead of
developing them. They also believe that talent
alone creates success, without effort. In a growth
mindset, however, people believe that their most
basic abilities can be developed through
dedication and hard work—brains and talent are
just the starting point. This view creates a love of
learning and resilience that is essential for great
accomplishment.

Understanding the differences between the
two mindsets and how the MOOC categorized
people into four types of resistance according to
their specific fixed mindsets have been
instrumental in my work as an instructional coach
and educational leader. This understanding allows
me to evaluate a teacher's resistance and respond
to them accordingly. Likewise, it helps me
support teachers who experience the same
situations with their students. I have worked with

both teachers and students who become resistant due to a fixed mindset because they are fearful; others resist because they feel inadequate. Of course, some are simply too comfortable—they have been set in their ways for a long time and feel that any change now would be unbearable. While all of these types of resistance from teachers and students are challenging to thwart, they can be transformed.

People can change their mindsets with any amount of help from others, or lack thereof. However, real meaningful change happens when someone decides to transform their *own* fixed mindset into a growth mindset. The work of a good coach, or teacher, is not forcing change upon someone but rather coaxing them to want to change something about himself or herself. At the end of the day, however, no one will change unless they see a need for it.

Change in the Time of Rapid Change

When I began my teaching career, the most advanced technologies I had available to me and my students were the chalkboard and the overhead projector. Our ideas of engaging lessons usually included ones where students were burying their noses in independent reading books

with little to no interaction or collaboration with
their classmates. Why did we think that the
quietest lessons were the ones that were the most
effective?

What I haven't even mentioned yet is that I
started teaching in 2006, and as hard as that is to
believe, that's what education was dealing with
even eleven years ago. Not long after that, not
only did educational technology take off, but so
did instructional methods and our appreciation
for, and search of, better ways to get students to
reach higher levels of engagement and
understanding. While things can change rapidly in
education, I am able to continue to provide
quality education to today's students because of
how I embrace changes when they occur, and
anticipate the ones that have yet to.

As an instructional coach, I have found
searching for ways to help shift people's minds to
be one of the most important parts of the job. It's
one that is not likely to be listed in a coach's job
description, or even that of a school- or district-
level administrator. It is, however, a necessary
evil of being a leader. Working with colleagues or
subordinates to grow their minds and help them
embrace change is never easy. It is equally
difficult, yet important, for classroom teachers to
be able to do the same with their students.

When I was hired as the instructional coach at my school, my administrators asked me to focus on two overarching areas: pushing the utilization of instructional technology (we were heading into the second year of one-to-one laptop initiative) and boosting the level of student engagement in the classroom. The subtle challenge there was to actually improve student engagement so much that it would improve the overall discipline at the school by driving down the growing number of student discipline referrals, suspensions, and expulsions. These goals and challenges could never have been attained or handled with fidelity by anyone until teachers' mindsets were preliminarily assessed and altered as necessary.

Why a Growth Mindset?

Last summer I attended an educational technology conference put on by the Leyden School District in Illinois. One of the keynote addresses was made by Josh Stumpenhorst, the 2012 Illinois teacher of the year, author, and trailblazing educator (his over 30,000 Twitter followers can likely attest to his influential thoughts and actions as an educator). In his address, he said something that completely resonated with me as someone who helps others to grow their mindsets to adapt to change and push education forward. When he began teaching, he simply needed to be more interesting than the squirrels and the trees outside his classroom window, yet he now has to be able to capture and hold the interest of today's students by being more interesting than YouTube and other technological distractions. Educators everywhere are finding that the teaching methods that were successful in getting us to learn new information when we were in school are no longer relevant, engaging, or effective anymore for modern students. That is why I have been a big believer in growth mindset for a long time.

Virtually all successful people - leaders, teachers, students, anyone - possess a growth mindset around many of the things they do. Conversely, those who hold fixed mindsets will never get beyond thinking that no matter what they do, they can never expect to see change, growth, or improvement. Those with growth mindsets push themselves to improve something because they do not want to remain stagnant or unsuccessful.

Dweck's research on growth mindset highlights this in that people with a growth mindset see their qualities as things that can be developed through their dedication and effort. Sure, they're happy if they're brainy or talented, but that's just the starting point, and this is where educators' mindsets need to be if they are to truly change their instruction to meet the needs of the students who are currently sitting in their classrooms. They must ensure that students are learning relevant material through relevant technology and other media, or other low-tech methods according to which works best for their students. They must allow the students to become immersed in the content to the point where *they* become the experts. They must allow students to reach higher levels of thinking and learning by synthesizing, analyzing, and creating content.

First, however, they must realize that there is a need to change based on something that has not been successful or remained stagnant for too long with little to no movement or growth whatsoever. That is why instructional coaching positions have popped up all over educational institutions across the country and across the globe. These professionals, like me, are tasked with the difficulty of getting teachers to find weaknesses in their students and themselves, then to plan and implement newer instructional methods that will be more successful. It's a dirty job, but someone has got to do it!

The Tragedy of the Comfort Zone

Another takeaway from a session I attended at the Leyden Symposium last summer was the term "TTWADI." Expanded, the term stands for That's the Way (I/We/They Have) Always Done It. That level of comfort is dangerous; while everyone likes to feel comfortable, it gets dangerous when it begins to hold people back from succeeding.

I like to think that we all have three "zones" that represent our willingness to change, or our growth mindset: the Comfort Zone, the No Zone, and the Grow Zone. As someone becomes comfortable with a practice, they are obviously in their Comfort Zone. Having to change, however, will require getting to the Grow Zone by way of the No Zone. Like the teachers I work with, or plenty of the students they work with, many people often need help navigating through the No Zone to reach the Grow Zone. Sometimes they are guided by new classroom management or instructional methods, sometimes by embracing newer technologies, and sometimes just by looking at a situation differently than before.

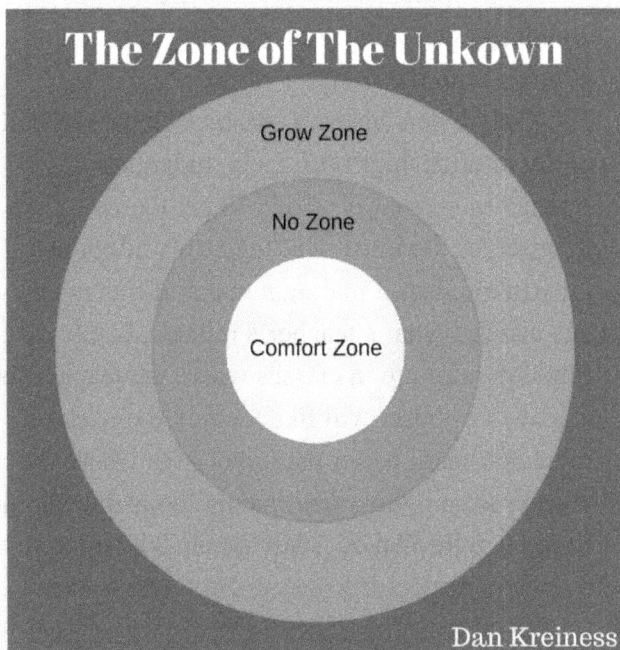

The Zone of The Unkown

Grow Zone

No Zone

Comfort Zone

Dan Kreiness

Unfortunately, the Comfort Zone is often where good ideas go to die. It's where people tend to get lazy and where once effective teachers lose their magic or mojo. Most unfortunately, the Comfort Zone is where students cannot learn in ways that resonate with them the most. When teachers stay in their Comfort Zone, it becomes too far removed from students' Comfort Zones. Teachers whose Comfort Zones still include the "drill and kill" style of instruction or the "sage on the stage" philosophy are often not able to relate to current students. Worse, they are not providing content in ways that students will relate to and connect with the best.

Only when teachers embrace change to build better relationships with their students and instruct them in ways that will get them to grow themselves the most, will they truly adopt a growth mindset. I maintain that students at any age can tell what a teacher's mindset is like. Students who are in classes where the teacher has a growth mindset will likely enjoy themselves more and learn better than in classes where the teacher is using instructional methods that should have been thrown out with the chalkboard and overhead projector from my 2006 classroom.

How to Grow your Mindset

Anyone, no matter how optimistic they are or how much of a growth mindset they possess, can also hold fixed mindsets about things as well. We can all point to times when we have felt that growth or change of any kind has become a task that was insurmountable, where we felt like we were driving through the longest tunnel ever built and could not see the light at the end of it. In combating this, Summer Howarth, the director of Edu Changemakers, an organization whose mission is to unleash teacher-led innovation, once said that "your why should make you cry." No one can change just because they are being asked to; they must know **why** they are changing.

One of the greatest leaders I know is a summer camp owner named Scott Rawls. Scott advises people who work for him at his camps to adopt an attitude that has them replace the words "I don't have to" with "I get to." Putting a growth mindset spin on that statement, instead of a teacher saying, "My principal told me I *have* to start using (insert new tech tool)" they would say "I get to start using (the new tech tool). Making subtle changes like that, and knowing the *why* behind the need to change something, makes it a much easier process.

I created a Voxer group last June as a session during Edcamp Voice. It quickly became one of the most active sessions during that edcamp, going almost nonstop for the nearly three days of the conference. Once the conference was over, not only did many of the group's participants convince me to continue it, they also remained active in the group.

As we continued to discuss the applications of growth mindset to education throughout the rest of the summer and into the new school year, I was even convinced to create the hashtag #growthmindsetedu and turn it into a monthly Twitter chat. While I'm proud of the work we've

done with the group, when I stand back and
reflect on why the group and Twitter chat have
such wonderful effects on participants, I can't
help but feel that there is still such a need for it in
education.

Become a Transformer in your School or Classroom

According to the same mindtools.com
article,[16] anyone can become a transformer.
Again, this can be done no matter what role
someone has, how old or experienced they are, or
even whether or not they have a leadership title. It
simply happens when someone recognizes the
need for a transformation and can inspire and lead
change efforts. The article says that people
become transformational leaders when they do a
few things: create an inspiring vision of the
future; motivate people to buy into and deliver the
vision; manage the delivery of the vision; and
build ever-stronger, trust-based relationships with
your people.

---

[16] (n.d.). Transformational Leadership - Leadership Training
from MindTools.com. Retrieved December 2, 2017, from
https://www.mindtools.com/pages/article/transformational-
leadership.htm

There will always be so many changes happening in education at any given moment in time. For instance, a while back we had to get used to educating students under the No Child Left Behind legislation, then we had to adapt to Common Core standards. Then last year No Child Left Behind was abandoned for the Every Student Succeeds Act.

Right now, we are also experiencing many changes within the realm of education technology and personalized learning. Because of all this change, it is vital that educators have the correct mindset when approaching anything new. Having a positive attitude and thinking about what's in students' best interest are great places to start.

The next time you or any educator you know is asked to change, start there. Realize the root cause for change. Wrestle with the intended audience and the conflicts they may face. Discover and uncover flaws in the system. That's all okay; it's part of the process. But without going through the process, without getting from the Comfort Zone through the No Zone and into the Grow Zone, change simply will not happen. If you can allow change to occur, and if you make growth happen, then you may know what it's like to have your why make you cry.

References

Burns, J. M. (1978). Leadership. New York: Harper & Row.

Dweck, C. S. (2006). Mindset: The new psychology of success. New York: Random House.

Mindtools.com. (n.d.). Transformational leadership: Becoming an inspirational leader. Retrieved from https://www.mindtools.com/pages/article/transformational-leadership.htm

Post, J. (2017). 11 ways to define leadership. Business News Daily. Retrieved from http://www.businessnewsdaily.com/3647-leadership-definition.html

About the Author

Dan Kreiness

Dan Kreiness is a middle school instructional coach in Connecticut. He began his teaching career in the New York City Department of Education as an English language arts teacher, academic intervention specialist, and middle-level literacy coach. Dan holds Master's degrees in adolescent education and educational leadership and is currently a doctoral student in the field of educational leadership. Dan is emerging as an expert presenter at education conferences, trainings, and edcamps on topics including leadership, growth mindset, student engagement, various instructional technologies, augmented and virtual reality for education, and using social media in education. Dan is the creator of the successful growthmindsetEDU Voxer group and

#growthmindsetEDU Twitter chat. He is an
ASCD Emerging Leader. Dan is also a Google
Certified Educator, Nearpod Pioneer, Flipgrid
Ambassador, and Hoonuit Learning Ambassador.

Dan features his writing on his own "Leader
of Learning" blog and has contributed guest blogs
to The EduCal Blog, Your Instructional Coach,
and TeachBoost. He was also a contributor to *The
EduMatch Teacher's Recipe Guide: Survive and
Thrive in the Kitchen and Beyond*. Dan has been a
recurring panelist on the EduMatch Tweet and
Talk podcast series and hosts his own "Leader of
Learning" podcast that can be found on iTunes or
Google Play.

Email Dan at *dan@leaderoflearning.com*.
Follow Dan on Twitter *@dkreiness*.

Engage to Empower

Engagement is key to school turnaround strategies.

The Error of Silencing Stakeholders: Community Engagement Reinforces School Turnaround Success

As school districts across the nation are working to turn around student and school success, the ways that families and communities are engaged within the process shapes the reach of success. In the book, *Bought Wisdom* by Dr.

JASON B. ALLEN: ENGAGE TO EMPOWER

Tony L. Burks,[17] he discusses success stories with schools that he's helped to turn around toward success. In one chapter, he mentions the power of, "Student-Centered Success Conferences with students and their families!"

In working with school districts around Metro Atlanta, I always give educational leaders the same spiel: "family and community engagement are the key to student and school success!" I say this because I want to encourage educational leaders to understand community and family engagement, specifically expanding their reach to the community, as its role in the academic achievement of students is critical.

---

[17] (n.d.). Bought Wisdom: Tales of Living and Learning (Volume 1): Dr. Tony .... Retrieved October 17, 2017, from https://www.amazon.com/Bought-Wisdom-Tales-Living-Learning/dp/0692871187

Understanding community engagement and its role in the academic achievement of students requires school leaders to be in tune, in touch, and in partnership with the communities they serve. I've heard a lot of principals in schools over the last couple of years say to parents, faculty, and staff, "we are here to serve students; that's our responsibility!"

Then, as the school year begins, they complain about student attendance, safe routes to school, or disgruntled students entering the doors in the morning. Well, when you're only focused on students within the school hours, you miss the critical factors that influence student performance such as family life, community dynamics (for example high poverty, crime, drug and gang violence rates), safe routes to school, and most importantly, community tragedies that happen.

All that affects how a student focuses, interacts, and engages while in school.

Community encompasses a group of people who live, learn, play, and fellowship/socialize together. Students live in neighborhoods, engage with family (immediate and extended), interact with sports and recreation teams, are members of clubs and organizations, attend faith-based institutions, and are engaged in common interests that all build a community.

School leaders can't have influence over communities they serve if they are not engaged. It's the same with elected officials. How can you serve me when you aren't aware of who I am, what I believe, what the issues are, and what those within the community have done to sustain, build, and heal the problems they collectively face? When I was matriculating through Atlanta Public Schools, principals and pastors were held in the same esteem. They worked together, collaborated on outreach initiatives, and had strong partnerships with the city, county, and school district leaders.

Everything that comes with change isn't always better. In recent years, there has been a clear distinction that there's an engagement issue between schools, communities, and families. In working with families and communities, many of them share the same experiences:

The school leaders don't know how to talk to us; they talk down to us like our children are a problem they can't solve. They make us feel like we should be doing all these methods and things they've tried at home that aren't working yet won't even have a conversation with us about what may possibly be working at school, in after-school programs, recreation centers or faith-based institutions. Ninety-eight percent of the time when faculty or staff call home, there's a problem. The 2% of good recognition is nine times out of 10 accompanied with a "but" or "while I have you on the phone!"

Members of the community sometimes feel neglected and overlooked as school leaders can make decisions regarding their community school and children without even concerning community plans, partnerships, and cultural dynamics. There are school districts who silence stakeholders in various forms from delaying information, ineffective communication, and providing poor customer service that turns stakeholders away. Utilizing communities and advocates for data, but not as partners, doesn't create trust. Talking about it, but not being about it, creates doubt and disengaged stakeholders.

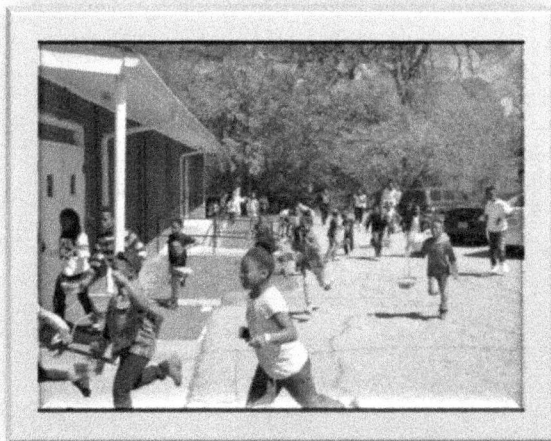

School districts can win with community engagement support! It begins with building trustworthy relationships. School districts, from school board members, superintendents, district, and school leaders, cannot build trustworthy relationships when they aren't focused on building children, families, and communities. So many districts make the mistake of solely focusing on support for students in turnaround strategies, and not looking at contributing factors to their ability to succeed or fail.

Family engagement is not the only factor that will ensure a student's success, but it plays a role. I've learned under the leadership of Dr. Karen

Mapp[18] that education is like baking a cake. She told the recipe for success which includes *good instruction* as the flour and *family engagement* as the baking soda. For schools to find success with school turnaround strategies, families and communities must effectively continue education at home. This can't be done without collaborative work. It's clear that without family engagement, the "Academic Cake[19]" will not rise.

A constructive way to engage communities in the turnaround process is to partner with them to help advocate for the work. *Understanding advocacy is key.* There will be many times that the leaders of education and stakeholders will not see eye to eye. How we handle disagreements is what strengths or destroys the work. I've witnessed educational leaders stereotype, downplay, disregard, and brush off educational advocates and stakeholders because they aren't speaking the same language. This most often happens when our focus is off.

---

[18] (n.d.). Karen L. Mapp | Harvard Graduate School of Education. Retrieved October 17, 2017, from https://www.gse.harvard.edu/faculty/karen-l-mapp
[19] (2015, November 2). A Parents' Night Recipe | Harvard Graduate School of Education. Retrieved October 17, 2017, from https://www.gse.harvard.edu/uk/blog/parents-night-recipe

As advocates, our focus for advocacy should be to bring awareness to needed areas of reform while ensuring the needs of children, families, and communities are being met by the school district which should coincide with the policies of the board and implementation district leaders. That sounds good, but here's the catch. Advocacy sustains accountability. It becomes problematic when leaders don't want to be held accountable, for example, when the funding sources for school districts, many coming from the private sector or corporations, want to follow their political agenda as opposed to the educational reform agenda. This creates pressure, tension, and disconnection between school districts and their stakeholders.

Advocacy from stakeholders is often feared and shunned because it drives accountability. It's often said that we have strict rules around how to hold our students and teachers accountable, but don't want the same accountability for the school district. Parents and stakeholders must be taught how to engage with school district leaders, just like they must be trained on how to navigate the school system. Building relationships with local advocates helps engage stakeholders on a deeper level that truly helps the growth and success of students and schools.

Here are some areas that school districts can partner with advocates and communities:

1) School beautification and clean-up days
2) Family and student crisis
3) Early learning and literacy
4) Clothes bank (school uniforms, sports/club uniforms, dance/prom, etc.)
5) Community garden and wellness
6) Mentoring and volunteer programs

The NAACP Youth & College Division had a slogan some years ago that simply states, *"Don't talk about it, be about it!"* This is what parents, students, and stakeholders are expecting from educators. Do what you say that you're going to do, which is to educate, empower, and equip our children with skills to succeed in our society. Time and time again, stakeholders have come to board and community meetings to hear the same thing. It's always "already done," "too late," and "nothing that we can do at this point except for the (insert the only option given to stakeholders that never truly benefits them)." We want leaders to be held accountable and to do what the vision says, what the plans are built around.

One of the most frustrating things parents have concerns about is that school districts make plans to do one thing and end up doing something else. "It's beyond a slap in the face, but a total disregard to our lives and our children," one Atlanta Adamsville parent stated in a community meeting about school closure. Parents found out in the second quarter of the school year that their school was suddenly being closed. When asked if it was because of academic performance, the answer was no, it was about finances. Decisions, statements, and outcomes like these are what make parents and stakeholders not trust the school district.

Here are actions that stakeholders want to see school districts do and not just say!

1) Engagement
2) Remediation
3) Restoration

Educational success lies in the ability of school districts to effectively engage stakeholders, build strong remediation paths, and restore the confidence of stakeholders through sound restorative justice practices. Parents want to know that they are a partner in the academic career of their child(ren). We must empower our parents to be at the table with their children, pre-K through 12. School districts must build stronger remediation plans.

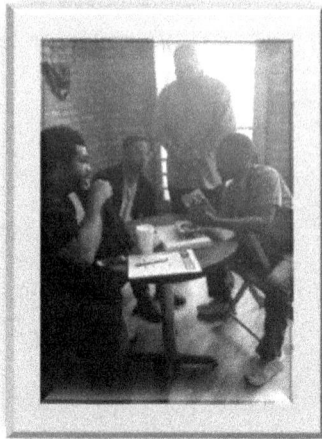

For two summers, I worked with summer school programs in our city's school district. It was a difficult process for parents. They received letters from the district, school, teacher, counselor, and just about anyone else working on student achievement data. Communication is successful when everyone is conveying the same message. Many of the parents automatically thought their children registered because of returning correspondence about summer enrichment. This example happens very often with schools and parents. How we communicate determines how we collaborate. Remediation programs through summer enrichment, after-school programming, or Saturday academies must be innovative, organized, and built around reaching the needs of students who are at risk of being left behind.

Communication makes our actions stronger. When people are informed, they can make better decisions about how they want to engage. Students can't afford to miss remediation support, so communication about this support heavily determines their future success. Remediation connects to restoration. Discipline across the board is a universal issue in education. How do we handle student management and discipline concerns effectively? It takes the village!

Restorative justice practices support student management and truly help develop our children socially, emotionally, mentally, and physically. While suspensions have only helped the growth of the school-to-prison pipeline, restoration helps schools turn the corner with academic progress. If students aren't in school, actively participating, focused, and engaged in the culture, then the school is doing nothing but preparing them for prison. Using restorative practices helps prevention initiatives with at-risk students, drives remediation, and reinforces each of our roles through engagement.

Finding Our Voices - The Call to Advocate: Advocacy Matters to School Turnaround

"The system was never designed for children that look like you to succeed. That's why it's important for you to beat the odds."

These were words that my great-grandfather would tell me as a child. My great-grandparents' childhood stories are filled with the history of our survival from slavery to freedom. They had a different value of education, homeownership, building a family, and serving your community, which I've come to learn are the important things to do as you seek success. As an advocate, the reason why I stand for equality and equity in education is because how we grow, learn, play, and engage shapes our minds, builds our character, and determines how we maintain relationships (business, personal, social, romantic, et cetera).

Reading is fundamental, it does take a village to raise a child, and education is the key to success. These themes aren't just catchy clichés. They are real. The level of education is a common denominator in the school-to-prison pipeline and the unemployment rate. However, we don't look at the importance of early childhood development as we should. The village concept is so critical to our success because what children see, hear, feel, and are exposed to in their early years stimulate their development. We must watch our behavior as adults, parents, and people of age around children.

This did not just begin in 2017! This generation of children is even bolder, even more vocal, more out of the box than those before them. They are aware of the social injustices happening around the world, happening to them. We can do a better job of hearing from, empowering, and engaging our children by doing it.

One of my teachers said something that changed my view of education: it's the light in the eyes that tells you who's won the battle between hope and hopelessness.

Regardless if you were gifted, talented, had special educational needs, SST, RPI, SEL, or behavioral challenges, what I remember from seeing my teachers do is ensuring that every child received the best education. They made sure they were engaged in the community, because they were the community. They lived in the community, they were aware of the effects of poverty, and were involved in helping change the economic deficits many of our communities faced.

Our teachers and school leaders showed us what entrepreneurship looked like, about the college experience, and why being an active alumnus is important. Students were encouraged to be leaders, innovators, thinkers, and achievers, and given a platform to *do*.

We must put our students in a seat at the table with student-led parent-teacher conferences, student-led discipline hearings, and more. We too often work to involve all stakeholders but leave the number one stakeholder out of the conversations.

For us to empower our students, we must empower teachers and staff. We don't often see top network series or sitcoms around teachers. Very rarely would television or movies portray teachers, professors, and educators on all levels, in every field, as heroes. We never see how teachers help build our economy, train the minds of our workforce, maintain our way of living, and change the continual challenges in the world.

With all of that said, there's a lot of drama, politics, power struggles in education. The challenge in equal pay and wages is an ongoing debate and struggle for school districts across the nation. Education is a life-changing career, not just a transitional job. Over the years I've seen more and more people come into the field because of assumptions and misinterpretations such as *it's easy work*, *they get summers off*, and *it's only working with children*. Matching these types of perspectives with the vast number of tasks given to teachers and educators, as well as the weight of being responsible for how children learn, grow, and become productive citizens isn't such a walk in the park, as many think.

In fact, the requirements, training, continuous professional development, and the required commitment for teachers isn't always reflected in their compensation. School districts do innovatively create additional ways for teachers to receive more compensation, but it is tied to more work. Doing after school, Saturday school, grant writing, or coaching adds more duties and takes away more time from teachers' personal lives. Teachers and educators need to have balanced lives like other professions, to ensure the physical, mental, and emotional well-being of their employees.

We cannot expect people to provide a service for us at the best quality when their personal and family lives are neglected. Having to neglect your own responsibilities doesn't increase work performance; in fact, it lowers it. Therefore, many school surveys from faculty and staff often reflect "poor" culture and climate. Many times, teachers and staff members feel like their voices aren't and can't be heard because of political strains, which create a culture of bullying and harassment. Compensation does not replace human respect and dignity. Regardless if the pay for teachers and educators is good, working under extremely stressful conditions often motivates people to do the bare minimum as opposed to performing in excellence. We need our teachers and educators to perform in excellence so that our students can reach their highest level of achievement.

Empowering parents helps to seal the deal for student success. Children will not reach their full potential if a strong support system isn't in place. It's also critically important for our faculty and staff to be prepared on how to engage and interact with the parents they serve. Regardless of if the parent's behavior is mimicked within the child(ren), we should hold a high standard of service to where we meet parents where they are, but also hold them accountable. There's a way to inform and include people not familiar with the school's culture. We can't label, target, or make assumptions about parents based on their zip code or level of education. We also must be mindful of how we talk to our parents and stakeholders. Everyone doesn't know all the educational acronyms that we use daily. Patience is the best virtue especially for those who work in administration and the front desk area.

Continuing Education at Home:
Engagement Matters to School Turnaround

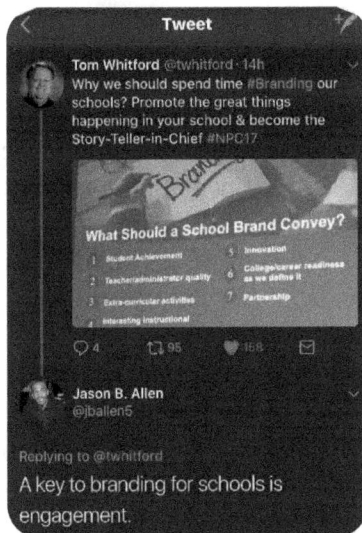

A key to branding for schools is engagement. Children aren't selecting Pre-K programs and registering for school; adults are. One of the things I share with schools whose family engagement programs I've supported is that parents want to know what the school can offer them, too. Engaging programs such as after school or early morning care, school clubs, organizations, and family building workshops attract parents to schools as partners and not just patrons. It creates an energetic partnership amongst all critical stakeholders in our students' education from parents, to administrators, support staff, and teachers. Family engagement is the key to school and student success and here's why:

1) Engaging families helps connect learning goals developed at home and school.
2) Supporting early learning development within communities builds stronger foundational support for Pre-K and early learning programs.
3) Ensuring families are engaged in college and career readiness, as well as adult educational advancement programs, builds culture and climate dynamics at both home and school.

Early development in a child's life is critically important to their learning abilities. Therefore, community and family engagement are so important to how our children, live, learn and play. Children need positive influences in their lives way before they enter the doors of our schools. I believe that even when our communities and families are unable to produce this, the school, as well as partners of education, should be there to support the village, as the village supports, rears, and protects the child. Everything that we do affects the development of our children from marriage sustainability and quality of food, to business and community development.

References

Burks, T., II. (2017, April 5). *Bought wisdom: Tales of living and learning (Volume 1)*. Retrieved October 17, 2017, from https://www.amazon.com/Bought-Wisdom-Tales-Living-Learning/dp/0692871187

About the Author

Jason B. Allen

Over the last 10 years, Jason B. Allen has worked in education servicing our students, families, and communities in various positions from Summer Camp Director, Teacher Assistant, and Associate Teacher, ELA & Reading Teacher (middle and high school), Parent Liaison, and Family Engagement Specialist. One of his major goals is to ensure that all youth have positive role models to emulate.

Throughout his academic career, he has mentored many young, African American males through his national mentoring program, BMWI (Black Men with Initiative), serving as the third National President. He has also volunteered with several community organizations including PTSA, Lillie's Foundation, Adoration Cares, and

the JoJo Martin Renal Disease Foundation. He
has served in various Board Chair capacities,
completed Board training through the GA Charter
Schools Commission, GA Leadership Academy
Economic & Leadership Development
Certification. He's also a YouCAN advocate with
50Can and a 2017 GA Forward fellow.

Embedding the spirit of service, the main
goal of Mr. Allen is to simply help others along
his life's journey. He is dedicated to servicing
those in need, determined to do the right thing for
the right reasons and dependable, living by his
word being his bond.

Techquity: How Technology Can Help Close the Opportunity Gap

Mason, M.Ed.

One educator's story on how living on the wrong side of the digital divide inspired him to find ways to bridge the gap using technology to transform teaching and learning

Living in the Gap

I did not always want to be an educator. Growing up, I thought I wanted to be a lawyer. I was a good student, inquisitive, articulate, and determined. And most of all, I loved to argue, defend my point of view, and win people over.

It's not uncommon growing up in an African-American household for parents, friends, and other relatives to encourage smart youth to become doctors and lawyers, so that seed was planted in me very early. However, I would come to realize that it was the seed I was willing to nurture, grow, and entertain throughout my life.

I grew up in Cleveland, Ohio, during the height of the crack cocaine epidemic and saw first-hand the effects of drug addiction, drug dealers, gang violence, and most importantly a struggling school system. I'm the oldest of eight children; my mother got pregnant with twins at 15-years-old. In order to provide and survive, my mother went on public assistance where she received welfare, food stamps, WIC, and public housing.

In addition to the mounting struggles of raising two young boys as high school dropouts, my mother and father became victims of the drug epidemic. As my mother battled her demons, she had to give up custody of my brother and me in the hope of getting clean. For approximately six years, my brother and I were fostered by my aunt, my mother's sister. Throughout that time, my mother's life was a living hell, but she was eventually able to win the battle over crack cocaine. My father, on the other hand, has never been as lucky, and to this day he is struggling with addiction.

Here's the thing about living in public housing, what most affectionately called the *projects*. They were never in good neighborhoods or near good schools. The achievement and opportunity gaps for me and most of the people I went to school with was very wide and very deep. Most of my peers who lived in my neighborhood and who went to my schools were African-American, of low socioeconomic status, and have similar stories to tell.

Consider the high school I attended. It was a dropout factory; it produced more high school dropouts than high school graduates. When I started as a freshman, we had ~400 students in our class, our sophomore year, that number dropped to ~300, by junior year, it was down to ~200, and when it was time to graduate, ~100 of us walked across the stage. That's right; we had a 75% chance of dropping out of high school!

I knew the odds were stacked against me growing up. Black -- strike one; poor -- strike two; struggling schools -- strike three. I was out before I even really began to play this game we call life; however, I saw how we lived, I saw how my mother struggled, and I saw how my neighborhood was crumbling around me. I knew I wanted more, and I knew the key to unlocking the door to the life I wanted to live was through education.

I learned very early on that I was a good student: listen to what the teacher said, follow the rules, do the work, and good grades would follow. I used to think perfect report cards with all As was a fairy tale, something that only happens to kids on television or in movies, to students who looked nothing like me, didn't have my background, and who didn't endure my struggles. Well, that was until fourth grade when I made straight As for the first time. I learned I could do it. I learned that it could be a reality. And I set out to do it every time.

I did eventually graduate high school with above a 4.0-grade point average, but I was the exception to the rule, and making the grade was only half the battle. I had to stay out of trouble, stay out of the streets, and figure out what my next steps were going to be. I participated in numerous extracurricular activities and sports to keep my nose clean.

It was my unwavering determination, perseverance, and what Robin Koval calls the four key ingredients to success: G.R.I.T. -- Guts. Resilience. Initiative. Tenacity (2015).[20] Despite every obstacle I faced in my life, I did not make excuses, I made it happen. Like Eric Thomas[21]

---

[20] (n.d.). Grit to Great. Retrieved October 15, 2017, from http://www.grittogreat.com/
[21] (n.d.). The Secret to Success: When You Want to Succeed as Bad as You .... Retrieved October 15, 2017, from https://www.amazon.com/Secret-Success-When-Succeed-Breathe/dp/B00B87A4KA

says, "When you want to succeed as bad as you want to breathe, then you'll be successful" (2011).

Closing the Gap

Many gaps exist in our education system and closing or bridging those gaps has been a daunting task. Unfortunately, as a student, I've been on the losing side of most of those gaps, including, but not limited to, the opportunity gap, the achievement gap, the discipline gap, the racial divide, and the digital divide.

The Schott Foundation for Public Education defines the opportunity gap as "the disparity in access to quality schools and the resources needed for all children to be academically successful" (2016).[22] When you place students in dropout factories with poor teachers and inadequate resources, the system is setting them up for failure. When I started as a high school student, I started the race already behind some of my counterparts. My opportunities were limited, and

---

[22] (n.d.). Opportunity Gap - Overview | Schott Foundation for Public Education. Retrieved October 15, 2017, from http://schottfoundation.org/issues/opportunity-gap/overview

I had to work extra hard to try to catch up and try to level the playing field.

The National Education Association defines the achievement gap as "the differences between the test scores of minority and/or low-income students and the test scores of their White and Asian peers" (2016)[23]. Affirmative Action tries to address the inequities in our education system, including bridging the achievement gap for minority students. I am thankful for Affirmative Action because, without it, I do not know if I would have been accepted to the university of my choice. Even though my grades were good, my scores on national standardized tests like the ACT and SAT were not as strong.

Gregory and Mosley[24] define the discipline gap "as a disproportionate disciplinary response to one race compared to others" (2004). In 2010, the U.S. Department of Education showed that 1 in 5 Black students was suspended compared to 1

[23] (n.d.). NEA - Achievement Gaps. Retrieved October 15, 2017, from
http://www.nea.org/home/AchievementGaps.html
[24] (n.d.). Gregory, A. & Mosely, M., (2004). The Discipline gap: Teachers' views .... Retrieved October 15, 2017, from http://gsappweb.rutgers.edu/rts/equityrsch/racialpdfs/GregoryMosely.pdf

in 20 White students.[25] Despite African-Americans being in the minority, their severe discipline rates have been in the majority nationwide. There are movements to right this wrong, including restorative discipline and culturally responsive teaching; however, I believe this was a major factor in the dropout rates of my peers at my high school.

The 1954 Supreme Court decision Brown v. Board of Education[26] overturned state-sponsored segregation in public schools; however, schools today still have a racial divide. The U.S. Government Accountability Office (GAO)[27] found that from the 2000-2001 to the 2013-2014, both the percentage of K-12 public schools in high-poverty and the percentage comprised of mostly African-American or Hispanic students grew significantly, more than doubling, from

---

[25] (2016, November 30). Civil Rights Data Collection (CRDC) - U.S. Department of Education. Retrieved October 15, 2017, from https://www2.ed.gov/about/offices/list/ocr/data.html
[26] (2017, September 14). Brown v. Board of Education National Historic Site (U.S. National Park .... Retrieved October 15, 2017, from https://www.nps.gov/BRVB/
[27] (n.d.). reformfinalpps | Top Down And Bottom Up Design | Education Reform. Retrieved October 15, 2017, from https://es.scribd.com/document/346663644/reformfinalpps

7,009 schools to 15,089 schools. The percentage of all schools with so-called racial or socio-economic isolation grew from 9% to 16%. Closing the racial divide is an American issue and must be addressed at all levels of our education system.

Lastly, Education World (2002) defines the digital divide as "the gap between students who have access to technology and students who don't.[28]" This is where my passion lies, and I believe if our education system is able to bridge the digital divide, it will help close the gap in many of these other areas of concern. That's where the marriage of technology and equity can help educators and our education system begin to transform teaching and learning.

Techquity

Technology and equity have been single for too long. Sure, they have gone on a few dates and talked about a long-term relationship, but the time has come for one of them to propose and make this relationship "'til death do us part."

---

[28] (n.d.). Education World: Caught in the Digital Divide | Digital Divide in .... Retrieved October 15, 2017, from http://www.educationworld.com/a_tech/tech041.shtml

Practitioners, policymakers, and other educational leaders all know the potential impact of technologies ability to close gaps; however, not all classrooms, schools, and/or districts are created equal.

In my career, I have worked in three different school districts from urban to suburban, and the differences in access were eye-opening. At the heart of the dilemma is equity work: how can we improve America's schools if we don't meet the unique and diverse needs of all students? And equity is different than equality. Every school does not need the same thing. Our schools that are economically disadvantaged need more than their wealthier counterparts.

That's where techquity comes into play: giving each classroom, school, and/or district the equitable distribution of technology to help all students reach academic success. This is a tall order considering how public schools are funded. This chapter is not about how to reform school funding; instead, I will make some suggestions based on my experiences as a classroom teacher, education technology instructional coach, and educational leader on how we can begin closing the digital divide through techquity.

Tackling the techquity conundrum involves a multilayered, multifaceted, and multidirectional approach to find solutions. However, if all education stakeholders do their part, techquity can be achieved. This includes action at the classroom at the classroom level, school level, and/or district level, and key players can include teachers, parents, administrators, colleges/universities, institutions, and organizations.

Teachers

When I started teaching, I was in a large urban school district, and like most teachers, I wanted to do what was best for my students. It is very well known that educators spend an inordinate amount of money to supplement resources in their classrooms. I actually took a second job to help buy materials for my middle school language arts classroom. I also used my own personal technology to help enhance teaching and learning in my classroom.

I don't expect educators to get second jobs to create techquity in their classrooms, but I would ask: what wouldn't you do to help level the playing field for your students? So, when I acquired the first iPad in 2010, I was immediately using that iPad in my classroom to help enhance my instruction. This early exposure to technology in the classroom exposed my students to what was possible in the classroom.

Nowadays, educators can use sites like Donors Choose or Support Your Local Teacher[29] to support innovations in their classrooms. Teachers have single-handedly helped close the digital divide for their students by getting tablets, laptops, digital cameras, robots, and other technology to fund the equity work in their classrooms.

Schools

I've worked at Title I schools, schools with high levels of poverty, which get additional financial assistance from the federal government. I've also worked in school districts with education foundations that allow educators to receive funds for special projects, initiatives, and technology in their classrooms or on their campus. These assets and how they are managed can make or break techquity efforts.

The two biggest hurdles in education are time and money, or better yet, what we do with our time and how we manage our money. The schools that see the biggest return on their investment are those that efficiently manage both time and

---

[29] (n.d.). Support Your Local Teacher. Retrieved October 15, 2017, from http://www.supportyourlocalteacher.org/

money. Title I schools can leverage their extra funds to close the digital divide on their campus by strategically investing in technology and professional development. Technology initiatives help meet the needs of most schools' mission and vision, and help with campus improvement goals.

I have been in several school districts that have education foundations. These foundations are not-for-profit extensions of the district who fundraise to support and enrich the district's mission and vision. Teachers are usually required to complete an application for a grant describing what they are requesting, why they are requesting it, and how it will help improve student performance. These applications can be time-consuming, and in my experience, most teachers won't fill out the application.

These are just two of the ways schools can work to close the digital divide through techquity at the campus level. Sometimes educators think that the change must come from the top down, but it can come from the bottom up. Every little effort makes a difference when striving for digital equity.

Districts

With funding inequities because of property taxes between rich school districts and poor school districts, the number one way schools can close the digital divide through techquity is through bonds. In 21st-century school settings, there is no reason why school districts aren't adequately preparing every student for the digital age. When establishing a bond, districts must leverage all forms of media to educate their constituents on the necessity of techquity.

Parents, students, and the community can all benefit from techquitable education reform. Technologies ability to transform teaching and learning and foster and enhance skills like communication, creativity, collaboration, and critical thinking help create a strong, diverse, and productive workforce. Students learn the hard and soft skills they need to succeed and thrive to support the local economic, political, and social infrastructures.

School, Family, and Community Partnerships

One of the best ways we can begin to close the digital divide and achieve techquity for our students is through school, family, and community partnerships (SFC). When everyone is working in one accord to do what's best for students in a 21st-century learning environment, mountains can be moved to achieve digital equity.

In the last public school district I worked in, I was proud to see an SFC partnership that was fostering digital innovation for students. It started with efforts from the municipal bond. After meeting with stakeholders for the schools, parents, and community, it was agreed that a one-to-one technology initiative would help close the opportunity gap for students in the district. This was a multilayered approach not tackled haphazardly, and had buy-in from all directions to improve the likelihood of success.

When everyone sets up their mind to close the gap, techquity is on the horizon. The school district decides to do the legwork needed to help its students compete, parents approve the bond that helps level the playing field, and the community does its part to provide resources, access, and support. Having devices and infrastructure in the schools is only half of the equation. Students need access to devices and infrastructure outside of school as well.

This district and the community recognized that needed to put systems in place to mitigate student access. Schools were left open on evenings to give students additional access to Wi-Fi, devices could be taken home, and if students did not have internet access, over 100 community partners opened their doors to students free of charge to access the internet outside of school. It is these types of efforts that help close the opportunity gap through techquity.

Government

In 2013, President Barack Obama announced the ConnectED Initiative,[30] which aims to connect 99% of students to high-speed internet. It is government initiatives like this that will help the United States education system reach techquity. This initiative provides training, devices, and the infrastructure for teachers and students across the country.

Future Ready Schools[31] (FRS) is another government-based initiative that helps district leaders across the nation recognize the potential of digital tools to bring techquity to their constituents. FRS provides frameworks for district leaders, technology leaders, coaches, librarians, and principals. These research-based frameworks help educators create innovative school cultures that can bridge the digital divide for all students.

---

[30] (n.d.). ConnectED - Office of Educational Technology. Retrieved October 15, 2017, from https://tech.ed.gov/connected/
[31] (n.d.). Future Ready Schools. Retrieved October 15, 2017, from http://futureready.org/

All school superintendents can take the Future Ready pledge, and other educators can attend meetups, webinars, institutes, and/or conferences to help them become Future Ready. This initiative strives to level the playing field for all students by closing the digital divide. It's up to us in the education community to take advantage of these free resources.

Corporations

Even companies are taking steps to help all schools reach techquity, including Digital Promise[32] and the Gates Foundation.[33] Digital Promise, in partnership with Verizon Innovative Learning,[34] has pledged to help close the digital learning gap. Bill and Melinda Gates Foundation's education division pledges to develop innovative solutions in education like digital equity.

---

[32] (n.d.). Digital Promise. Retrieved October 15, 2017, from http://digitalpromise.org/
[33] (n.d.). Gates Foundation. Retrieved October 15, 2017, from https://www.gatesfoundation.org/
[34] (2017, October 5). Verizon Innovative Learning | Verizon. Retrieved October 15, 2017, from http://www.verizon.com/about/responsibility/verizon-innovative-learning

When companies like Apple, Google, Microsoft, and Verizon assist in closing the opportunity gap, they help remove one of the largest barriers to techquity: money. Schools and districts must be made aware of these opportunities, take advantage of them, and foster cultures of transformation and innovation through technology integration. Then they will be closer to digital equity and give all their students an opportunity for success.

Leading in the Gap

As an educational leader, in the last year, I have learned more than anything is to mind the gap. Like the warnings that greet patrons at the London Underground, not minding the gap could have dire consequences. If practitioners, policymakers, and other stakeholders do not mind the techquity gap, it will have consequences for our neediest students.

These are just a few ways schools, districts, educational organizations, companies, and institutions can begin bridging the digital divide. Technology not only has the potential to level the playing field for disadvantaged students, but it can also help them rise above their peers.

Growing up, I was not afforded the same opportunities as my more affluent counterparts: I did not go to the best schools, have the best teachers, or the best resources. Let's change this paradigm of systemic inequity and help all students not only survive but thrive in this rapidly changing world.

References/Resources

Education World (2002). Caught in the Digital Divide http://www.educationworld.com/a_tech/tech041.shtml

Gregory, A. and Mosely, P. (2004). *The Discipline Gap: Teachers' Views on the Overrepresentation of African Americans in the Discipline System.* Equity and Excellence in Education, 37, no.1: 18- 30, Education Research Complete.

National Education Association (2016). Students Affected by Achievement Gaps http://www.nea.org/home/20380.htm

Thaler, L. K., & Koval, R. (2015). *Grit to great: how perseverance, passion, and pluck take you from ordinary to extraordinary.* New York: Crown Business.

Thomas, E. (2011). *The secret to success: when you want to succeed as bad as you want to breathe*. Atlanta: Spirit Reign Pub.

U.S. Department of Education, "Civil Rights Data Collection," March 2012, accessed http://www2.ed.gov/about/offices/list/ocr/docs/crdc-2012-data-summary.pdf.

U.S. Government Accountability Office (2016). Better Use of Information Could Help Agencies Identify Disparities and Address Racial Discrimination https://assets.documentcloud.org/documents/2838279/GAO-Segregation-Report.pdf

About the Author

Mason, M.Ed.

Mason, M.Ed. is an Education Technology National Instructor with EdTechTeacher, Inc. and an Ed.D. student at Southern Methodist University studying PreK-12 Educational Leadership. He is passionate about helping educators transform teaching and learning through technology integration and closing the digital divide through equitable access to technology for all students.

Mason obtained his B.A. in English and Education from Ohio State University and his M.Ed. in Educational Leadership from Southern Methodist University. He taught secondary English, Language Arts, and Reading for eight years in Dallas ISD and Plano ISD, and spent a year as an Education Technology Instructional

Coach at a 9-12 one-to-one iPad high school in Garland ISD. His passion for improving teaching and learning has guided his work in schools across the nation and various local, regional, and national conferences.

Analog Love

J. Derek Larson

As amazing as technology is, sometimes we need to unplug to truly connect with one another.

This was originally published on www.EdTechBabble.net and has been modified from its original version.

There is something very nice about being able to "unplug" from technology and return to nature. One of my family's favorite traditions is to go up to my in-laws' cabin and get away for a weekend or two each summer. We love it so much, we always try for 2-3 visits per year, if not more.

Now, this isn't a cabin that is more house-like with all the major amenities like satellite T.V., Internet connectivity, paved roads, et cetera...this is a rugged cabin where, yes, there is power and plumbing, but that's about it. We have to travel up a bumpy dirt trail (I guess it is a road), but it's not frequently graded by the city or county, so it feels more trail-like. Then we finally arrive at this, a wonderful relaxing break from all things "connected" for the duration of our stay.

One of my favorite parts of going to the cabin is the chance to truly unplug and not worry about my email, current RSS subscriptions I haven't had a chance to read, or other online planning for events I'm involved with. Instead, I can take an opportunity to sit back and enjoy some family time. My kids know they can't play on the iPad, which usually means watching a few episodes of their favorite PBS Kids shows. They are perfectly fine with it because they get to explore some of the awesome nature! We hike, throw rocks in the creek that flows by the cabin, pick wildflowers, and play card games (after little sister goes to bed, so she doesn't try to eat/destroy the cards). We have a blast, and I really miss it all once we head back down the mountain to civilization.

The amazing Jon Spencer (@edrethink) once wrote a piece entitled, "There's No App for That," which has since been removed. He mentioned that his family has designated off-screen times and that it forces them to interact with the "real world" and not just the online fun that we create for ourselves.

What is his reason for being so hard on his family and not allowing them the freedom to be creative in a digital manner?

> "I want them to know that the world is round."

What? Can't you learn that from Wikipedia or a Google search or looking at online pictures? Yes, all those things can help one to learn about the world, but here's an even better way to learn about the world, *go live in it*!

Go explore. Go outside and play. Go outside and play with others and learn what the world "feels" like, what it "smells" like, what it "tastes" like (I do not condone the act of eating things that will either make you sick or kill you, but a little dirt or grass here or there is good for you, right?), and enjoy the "real world," not just through pictures.

Jon goes on to talk about the fact that his kids play pretend, and even get into sibling fights over nothing important, but the typical sibling fights. But one of the absolute best lines in the entire post was his last line,

> "it was augmented reality in a way that you can't find on a screen."

I love technology and all the amazing things it can do you us and education, but it can't show us the real-world things of this world better than actually going outside and living can.

With all of this said, I think I we need to spend some time remembering some of the great things in this life that aren't digital. I love a lot of analog tools; in fact, I am frequently asked to speak to groups of educators about some of my favorite tools I use daily.

I typically can't help but talk about my favorite index cards (yes, I have favorites) and one of my favorite pens (yes, you read that right, pens, as in multiple favorites). I blame Myke Hurley (@imyke) and Brad Dowdy

(@dowdyism)of the Pen Addict Podcast[35] for this one. Go listen and you'll see why).

Many of those in attendance often seem a little confused because I am the "tech guy" and yet I'm talking about analog stuff. Yep, and I can't help it. Some of my most used tools are, in fact, analog and I *love* it! I hope you'll be willing to get out there and give analog tools a try. You never know, they may become some of your favorite tools too!

---

[35] (2013, March 13). The Pen Addict Podcast - Now With More 5by5 — The Pen Addict. Retrieved December 2, 2017, from https://www.penaddict.com/blog/2013/3/13/the-pen-addict-podcast-now-with-more-5by5

About the Author

J. Derek Larson

Husband, father, teacher, learner, tech addict, musician, and friend.

J. Derek Larson taught 4th and 5th grades in Southern Utah for 8 years, absolutely loving every minute, before becoming the Educational Technology Director for the Southwest Educational Development Center (SEDC) in Cedar City, Utah.

Having completed his M.Ed. with an emphasis on technology, he feels technology is one of the most crucial aspects of teaching because of the way students are excited by and look forward to using it. If educators can find ways to effectively harness technology into their teaching, they will be better able to reach their students and help them catch the excitement of learning. This is one of Derek's goals as he works with teachers in rural districts across Southwestern Utah.

He was awarded the 2014 UCET Outstanding Young Educator of the Year. He also received the Certified Educational Technology Leader (CETL) certification from the Consortium for School Networking (CoSN) in October of 2016. Earning the CETL certification helps education technology leaders demonstrate they have mastered the knowledge and skills needed to define the vision for and successfully build 21st-century learning environments in their school districts.

Derek is a moderator for #UTedChat, an education Twitter chat focused on Utah educators which happens every Wednesday @ 9pm MDT. Come on by and join the conversation; non-Utahans are welcome as well.

He is serving his fifth year as a member of the UCET Board where he is the currently working as the Public Relations Director.

Derek has three kids and a wonderful wife who help him stay grounded in the things that matter most. He loves spending time with them in the mountains, where he is reminded of the need to unplug occasionally to make sure he is the best person he can be.

Standards for Teaching in Ghana

Miracule Gavor

Standards for teaching in Ghana

Over the years, Ghana has reformed and restructured its teacher education system in response to demands of a new vision and mission for education to meet the demands of a knowledge society. What has been missing in this entire process is a set of professional standards for teachers, which provide a strong definition of and a key reference point for the work of teachers towards achieving the learning and social outcomes articulated in the 2008 Education Act. The Standards are therefore designed to codify what a "good teacher" looks like for Ghana, recognizing the urgent need to improve the quality of the school experience and learning outcomes for all learners and to raise the status of teachers in their communities and country.

The Standards are aspirational in their vision, positively embracing the promises and challenges of the 21st century for Ghana. Importantly, they support Ghana in meeting Goal 4 of the

Sustainable Development Goals for 2030[36] to "ensure inclusive and equitable quality education and promote life-long learning opportunities for all." In contributing towards this Goal, the Standards are also, however, realistic, and relatively few in number to be achievable and user-friendly.

Development of the Standards was also informed by a review of international teaching standards. What is deemed most important is that teachers apply their content knowledge in the classroom, thereby demonstrating sound pedagogical content knowledge. Correspondingly, the practicum within teacher education programs can comprise up to 25 percent of the course.

Taking the existing Ghanaian standards, aims for teacher education, context, and the international standards into account, these new Standards for Ghana emphasize the applied, practical work of a teacher as a valued professional in a community of practice. They also envisage a warm and friendly teacher who has secure curricular, subject, and pedagogical content knowledge, who plans for and uses

---

[36] (n.d.). Education - United Nations Sustainable Development. Retrieved December 2, 2017, from http://www.un.org/sustainabledevelopment/education/

differentiated interactive instructional strategies and resources and so engages their learners, and who achieves higher learning outcomes for all (particularly learners who are more vulnerable, such as those with disabilities, girls, and students identified as gifted). The Standards also call for a purposeful use of assessment productively in achieving those outcomes.

How are the Teaching Standards Organized?

The standards are divided into three main domains, each with its own sub-divisions.

Professional Values and Attitudes

Professional Development
Community of Practice

Professional Knowledge

Knowledge of Educational Frameworks and Curriculum
Knowledge of Learners

Professional Practice

Managing the Learning Environment
Teaching and Learning
Assessment

These three domains and aspects encompass what teachers should value, know, and do. Furthermore, they intersect to help develop a competent teacher, by the time they have reached the end of their three year-initial teacher training.

About the Author

Miracule Gavor

As a mathematics educator, Miracule led various mathematics projects and workshops for students and teachers at pre-tertiary level across Ghana since 2008. Most of these projects focused on engaging academically challenged schools and students in collaborative mathematics workshops, as well as the design and piloting of activity-based mathematics concepts, development of numeracy approaches, and review of mathematics curriculum.

As the National Math Coordinator for USAID Partnership for Education: *Learning,* and a former Basic Schools Representative with the Ghana Mathematics Society, he collaborated to create and instructed practical mathematics courses for students and teachers all over Ghana that were specifically geared towards revamping mathematics education.

Miracule is currently working with a team of 10 other math specialists on developing a new math curriculum for Ghana through the National Council for Curriculum and Assessment.

Better and Better

Sarah Thomas

Regardless of what lies ahead, we are always looking to grow our family. Thank you for being part of it.

September 2017

It seems like every year gets better and better. We are a little over three weeks away from the third birthday of EduMatch, and the 100th episode of Tweet & Talks. In 2017, we've had so much to celebrate in the group, such as job promotions, awards, and new additions to the families of EduMatch members. As a group, we embarked on a new journey together with the launch of *#EduMatch Snapshot in Education* (Thomas et al., 2016) last December, and *The EduMatch Teacher's Recipe Guide: Survive and Thrive in the Kitchen and Beyond* (Neil et al., 2017) in June.

We had two official meetups this year, EdCamp EduMatch (www.edcampedumatch.org) online and one face-to-face at ISTE in San

Antonio. (In the ISTE highlight reel[37] played during the closing keynote, we even see many of our members making cameo appearances!)

For the past three years, ISTE events have always been a highlight of EduMatch, even for those of us who participate through #NotatISTE. This year, a team of #PasstheScopeEDU members (See Lewis in Thomas et al., 2016, pp. 199-214) live-streamed several sessions, making the experience even more vivid for EduMatchers who were not physically present, but there with us in spirit. I was very inspired and moved by my ISTE experience this year, as I saw several themes emerge, which aligned with our mission for EduMatch.

According to the Community Guidelines:[38]

---

[37] (2017, July 17). ISTE 2017 Conference & Expo Highlights - YouTube. Retrieved October 3, 2017, from https://www.youtube.com/watch?v=zTGKWWDi4JA
[38] (n.d.). Community Guidelines - EduMatch®. Retrieved October 3, 2017, from http://www.edumatch.org/community-guidelines

> We are a worldwide community of educators who **learn and grow together**. We support one another in our professional learning journeys, and believe in the **power of sharing stories**. For that reason, we connect on various social media platforms and **build deep relationships** that transcend geography, job titles, and all demographic categories. We also believe in empowering the expert within, and seek to amplify voices of students and educators, as well as grassroots educational efforts. (emphasis added)

Granted, this mission statement was crafted shortly after ISTE 2017, but it was assembled from several blog posts, interviews, and other sources curated throughout our two years in existence. After ISTE, the stars aligned, and the mission almost seemed to write itself. In this chapter, I will deconstruct this mission through the lens of ISTE 17 and other relevant experiences.

Learning and Growing Together

Somehow, the default catchphrase I use when welcoming someone to either of our EduMatch Voxer groups is, "we look forward to learning and growing with you." This is not lip service, as I have learned more in my four years of being connected than I have in the previous nine as an educator. The key word in this subheading is "together." Yes, I am a lifelong learner; however, left to my own devices, I won't get as far. Learning with others provides me with that social aspect that I secretly crave, but am sometimes uncomfortable to do in face-to-face settings. Also, I am gently held accountable by my PLN, comprised of individuals with the same desire to grow professionally.

Recently, I have been pleased to see many renowned organizations such as ISTE (Educator Standard 1, 2016), Future Ready, and the Office of EdTech (2015, p. 34) place such a high emphasis on personalized professional learning. I was very excited to interact with all three of these organizations within the past year, as a symposium attendee of the Office of EdTech in 2016, a Future Ready National Advisor for the Coaches' Strand, and a member of the Technical Working Group for the ISTE Standards for Educators refresh.

In working on the new Standards for Educators, the first standard, Learner, resonated most with me, particularly indicator 1b: "Pursue professional interests by creating and actively participating in local and global learning networks." This is what "learning and growing together" is all about. This is my jam!

This was also the topic of my ISTE ignite, which I did before the opening keynote. This was a major highlight of my career! I was terrified, but excited to share about the amazing things that I have learned from all my friends in EduMatch, and other networks. Initially, I had planned to cover all the standards by showing a crowdsourced presentation from our community, about how they embodied the new standards (getconnected.edumatch.org/istestandards). However, the scope was too broad for five minutes, so my friends at ISTE suggested that I focus on Standard 1, and share the story of my good friend Anibal Pacheco

(@AnibalPachecoIT), as well as more about EduMatch.

I remember being very anxious backstage, and I decided to Periscope to calm my nerves (events.edumatch.org/backstageatiste). Soon, I heard Richard Culatta, CEO of ISTE, begin to introduce me. I took a deep breath and went on autopilot. The video of the ignite is at presentations.sarahjanethomas.com/isteignite2017.

Deep Relationships

One unexpected takeaway from my presentation was an accidental acronym, the PLF. In my revised focus, I tried to speak from the heart as to what the connections facilitated through EduMatch and other networks meant to me. The best possible fit was the word "family," which I mentioned in passing in last year's edition of this book (Thomas et al., 2016, p. 258). In the ignite, I discussed how lucky many people are to build a professional learning network, and to find their tribe; however, I have been truly blessed with finding family.

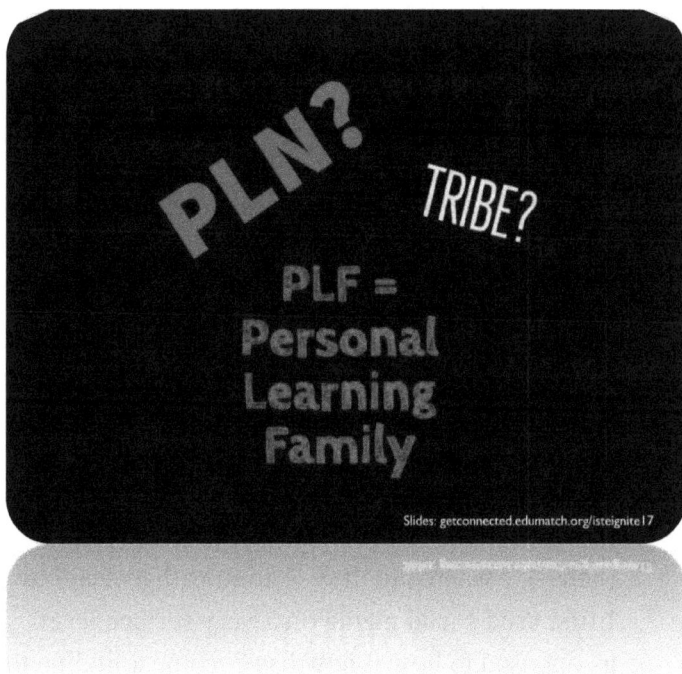

I realized that when these connections go beyond simple networking, we are able to have conversations that truly matter. Deeper connections allow for us to understand why others think or believe the way they do, and we can approach difficult conversations with love, empathy, and respect. These often lead to resolution, or at a minimum, a greater understanding.

I love telling stories of how I have been able to connect with other educators through technologies such as YouTube Live and Voxer, to the point that when we first meet offline, it feels like we have grown up together. The second time, I may be coming to their house for dinner, or even sleeping in their spare bedroom (or vice versa). Surface conversations are fine, but we have to be open to digging deeper if we really want to connect and understand others.

Funny story...I was sitting backstage checking my notifications at ISTE after the ignite, and I began to see #PLF popping up. My first reaction was honestly...confusion lol. My intention was not to create a new acronym, as I think we have way too many of those already (haha!). I wanted to draw a contrast between how I first used social media on a very surface level, as opposed to how it now has become a lifeline to some people I love (but may not have even "met" in the traditional sense).

I was afraid that I had accidentally branded this very complex emotion *into just another hashtag*; however, the more I spoke to people and listened to their stories, the more I realized that we shared the same feelings. So, now I embrace it and thank my PLF for pouring into me so much over the years.

Sharing our Stories

There is no magical pill to building these deeper connections; instead, it comes as a result of time, trust, and vulnerability. Sharing our stories is extremely important in the latter two factors. One major highlight of #ISTE17 was Tuesday morning when I listened to friends Clara Alaniz (@techclara) and Jennie Magiera (@MsMagiera) deliver their ignite and keynote, respectively.

In her ignite, Clara shared about growth in our students using several personal examples including examples from her own family (we joked afterward about her extended metaphor using cilantro). Next, Jennie took the stage and blew my mind with her vulnerability, and advocacy for educators to share their stories, for better and for worse. My takeaway is that we need to be vulnerable and open to laugh together, to cry together, to celebrate together. All these are equally important, and *all* voices need to be heard.

It's not a secret that I am not a fan of popularity contests we sometimes see in education. We've had many conversations in EduMatch about this. We are all working together to be our best, so that we can do our best. Everyone is important in this work, and if anyone needs to be placed on a pedestal, it is our students. This year at ISTE, I loved the recurring theme that everyone has a story to share and that we should all be open to listening to and learning with one another.

What Lies Ahead

What makes EduMatch work is the fact that people bring a piece of themselves with them as they join. We are constantly adapting, trying new ideas, and pushing the boundaries of what we thought we were capable of. But as they say on the old hair commercials, "I'm not only the president, I'm also a client." Here is what I hope to see in the future.

First, you can expect to see more publications from EduMatch Publishing. These include crowdsourced anthologies such as this, as well as some solo projects. Also, I am greatly looking forward to our fourth annual ISTE meet up in Chicago. Also, we just rolled out a badging system to extend our learning even further. We may even expand Edcamp EduMatch to include a physical component in 2018. Finally, we just submitted paperwork to open a nonprofit arm of EduMatch, *EduMatch Foundation, Inc.* This will bring forth many exciting changes in 2018 and beyond. Stay tuned!

Regardless of what lies ahead, we are always looking to grow our family. Thank you for being part of it.

References

Neil, T., Thomas, S., Ball, D., Brady, T., Casa-Todd, J., & Cate, C. (2017). *The EduMatch teacher's recipe guide: Survive and thrive in the kitchen and beyond.* Woodbridge, VA: EduMatch.

Thomas, S., Simmons, T., Poth, R. D., Pierson, R. J., Harris, B., Ward, R. et al. (2016). *EduMatch: Snapshot in education (2016).* Woodbridge, VA: EduMatch.

U.S. Department of Education, Office of Educational Technology. (2015). *Future ready learning: Reimagining the role of technology in education.* Retrieved from https://tech.ed.gov/files/2015/12/NETP16.pdf

About the Author

Sarah Thomas

Sarah-Jane Thomas, PhD is a Regional Technology Coordinator in Prince George's County Public Schools. Sarah is also a Google Certified Innovator, Google Education Trainer, and founder of EduMatch.

Sarah was designated an ASCD Emerging Leader in 2016, and was named by the National School Board Association as one of the "20 to Watch" in 2015. She was also part of the Technical Working Group that refreshed the International Society for Technology in Education (ISTE) Standards for Educators in 2016-2017, and in 2017, she received the ISTE "Making IT Happen" Award.

EduMatch Snapshot in Education (2017)
Volume 2: Professional Practice

Visit us at edumatch.org

Coming Soon: Snapshot in Education 2018
Now seeking interested authors. Please inquire at
books.edumatch.org/edusnapinterestform.

Other EduMatch Books

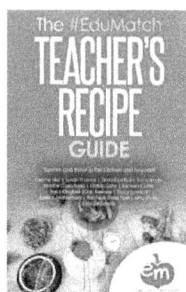

In this collaborative project, twenty educators located throughout the United States share educational strategies that have worked well for them, both with students and in their professional practice.

Hey there, awesome educator! We know how busy you are. Trust us, we get it. Dive in as fourteen international educators share their recipes for success, both literally and metaphorically! In this book, we come together to support one another not only in the classroom, but also in the kitchen.

www.ingramcontent.com/pod-product-compliance
Lightning Source LLC
Chambersburg PA
CBHW060010050426
42448CB00012B/2687